HOW TO USE

Netscape Communicator 4.0

HOW TO USE

Netscape Communicator 4.0

Rebecca Tapley

Ziff-Davis Press
An imprint of Macmillan Computer Publishing USA
Emeryville, California

Publisher	Joe Wikert
Associate Publisher	Juliet Langley
Acquisitions Editor	Lysa Lewallen
Development, Copy Editor	Margo Hill
Technical Reviewer	Bryan Hiquet
Production Editor	Carol Burbo
Proofreader	Tim Loughman
Book Design	Dan Armstrong
Page Layout	M. D. Barrera
Indexer	Thomas McBroom

Ziff-Davis Press, ZD Press, and the Ziff-Davis Press logo are trademarks or registered trademarks of, and are licensed to Macmillan Computer Publishing USA by Ziff-Davis Publishing Company, New York, New York.

Ziff-Davis Press imprint books are produced on a Macintosh computer system with the following applications: FrameMaker®, Microsoft® Word, QuarkXPress®, Adobe Illustrator®, Adobe Photoshop®, Adobe Streamline™, MacLink® Plus, Aldus® FreeHand™, Collage Plus™.

Ziff-Davis Press, an imprint of
Macmillan Computer Publishing USA
5903 Christie Avenue
Emeryville, CA 94608

ISBN 1-56276-467-5

Manufactured in the United States of America
10 9 8 7 6 5 4 3 2 1

This book is dedicated
to Steve.

_____

MANY THANKS to Lysa Lewallen for patiently answering *all* of my questions, to Margo Hill for helpful insights and lots of renumbering, to Carol Burbo and Pipi Diamond for organizing and shepherding all the content, and to Madhu Prasher and all the other people at Ziff-Davis Press who labored to make this book the best it could be. Thanks to Ziff-Davis's production team for all their hard work, to Brian Hiquet for technical editing and assistance above and beyond the call of duty, and to Nancy Warner for taking all these screen shots! Finally, thanks to Chris Van Buren, Cathy Elliott, and Waterside Productions for making it easier for me to do what I do.

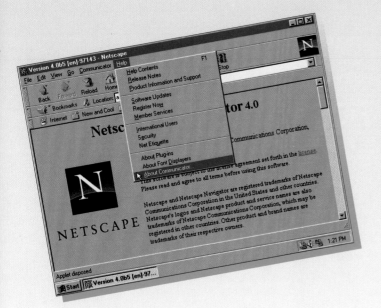

O F C O N T E N T S

PART 3

Using Messenger: Managing E-Mail

PART 4

Using Collabra: Participating in Newsgroups

INTRODUCTION

YOU'VE HEARD ABOUT the Internet's World Wide Web. You've heard about Web sites, surfing the Web, commerce on the Web, and much, much more—and if you're like the millions of people who buy computers and subscribe to Internet accounts every year, now you're curious and want to get involved.

You may also already have a computer and/or a previous version of Netscape Navigator. You may have lots of experience with other computer programs because of your job, or some experience because your kids have a computer at home or at school. Either way, you're also curious and you also want to get involved.

This book is for anyone, experienced and inexperienced, who wants to learn all about Netscape Communicator.

With this book and the Communicator software, you have an unprecedented opportunity to explore every nook and cranny of the Internet. You may have seen other How to Use books about Netscape Navigator, but this book contains much, much more—Netscape Communicator is a *suite* of *five* programs.

Netscape Navigator is the central piece of the Communicator pie as the Web browser, but the other parts are just as intriguing. Netscape Messenger is a complete e-mail management system with sophisticated sorting, tracking, and saving features that allow you to

make the most of your online communications. In this book, you'll learn about how to use e-mail more effectively to make the most of your valuable time.

Netscape Collabra connects you to the vast network of newsgroups, thousands of online discussion groups about any subject you can think of—for any hobby, pastime, or interest you have, there's a newsgroup for it, and Collabra will find it for you. This book introduces you to the world of newsgroups, helps you find what you're looking for, and teaches you the rudiments of newsgroup posting, participation, and etiquette.

Netscape Composer is the second-generation Web page authoring tool that goes far beyond Navigator Gold; its tools and capabilities make it possible to create cutting-edge Web pages without having to learn all the cutting-edge technologies. With Composer, you can create Web pages with templates or with the magical Web Page Wizard, or you can go it alone with just you and the tools—Composer gives you room to grow.

Finally, Communicator gives you a glimpse of the Web's immediate future with Netscape Conference: With Conference, you can make a long distance phone call to any other Communicator user anywhere in the world, for just the cost of your Internet connection. There are no long distance company charges by the minute, and there's no difference between calling Chicago or China. With Conference, you can stay in touch and talk longer.

In short, Communicator's like nothing else you've ever seen, even if you're using an older Netscape product.

How to Use Netscape Communicator 4.0 is an intelligent introduction and a helpful tutorial for people who want to learn step by step without lots of technical talk, assumptions, or condescension. If you have a computer and a modem, this book will take you through the entire process from helping you download Communicator from Netscape's Web site, to teaching you how to receive e-mail and newsgroup postings, to showing you how Communicator uses plug-ins and security features.

PART 1

Getting Started: Exploring Navigator

NETSCAPE NAVIGATOR is a Web browser, a software application that allows you to access information on the Web in a graphical, easy-to-use format. Just as you need a vehicle to drive on the highway, you need a Web browser to browse, or surf, the Web.

Simply put, browsers retrieve information from other computers and bring this information to your computer. This information can be just about anything—text, graphics, sound files, software, movies—and can exist on any computer anywhere in the world that is connected to the Internet.

IN THIS SECTION YOU'LL LEARN

How to Install Communicator

Your first—and one of the easiest—tasks is to install Navigator on your desktop PC. After you've turned on your computer, starting Windows 95, you'll see the Component taskbar at the bottom of your display. To the far left of this taskbar is a button labeled Start. From here you'll install Navigator, which is contained on a CD-ROM. During the installation you'll be asked whether you'd like to install Navigator using Typical or Custom options. For our purposes, the Typical option works best. You'll then restart Windows and, having installed Navigator successfully, you'll be well on your way to Web wandering.

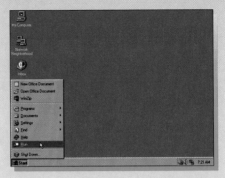

1 After you've turned on your computer and launched Windows 95, put the Netscape CD-ROM in the CD-ROM drive. Click the Start button in the lower left corner of your screen and select Run from the menu.

8 Setup is complete. Click OK to return to your desktop, where you'll see the Netscape Communicator icon. This is the icon you'll click to start Communicator.

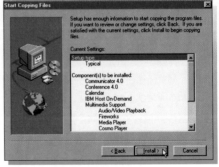

- Before you lay the groundwork to connect to the World Wide Web, you'll want to be sure your desktop PC meets the system requirements for Communicator. The minimum requirements for Windows 3.1 are a 386/33 CPU, 4MB RAM, and 10MB hard disk space. If you have Windows 95, you'll need a 486/66 CPU, 8MB RAM, and 10MB hard disk space. You'll also need a 14.4Kbps data/fax modem, although a faster 28.8Kbps modem is recommended.

7 Check your current settings one more time and click Install to begin installing Communicator's program files on your hard drive. A progress dialog box will appear so that you can follow Communicator's progress.

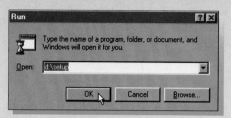

2 Now the Run dialog box will appear. Place the cursor in the text box, click once, and type in **d:/setup**, replacing what's already written if necessary. Click OK, and you'll automatically be taken to the Netscape Communicator Setup screen.

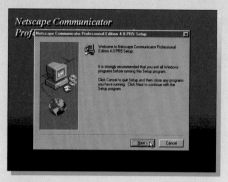

3 If you haven't exited all other Windows programs before starting setup, click Cancel and do so before beginning installation again. If you're ready to install Communicator now, click Next.

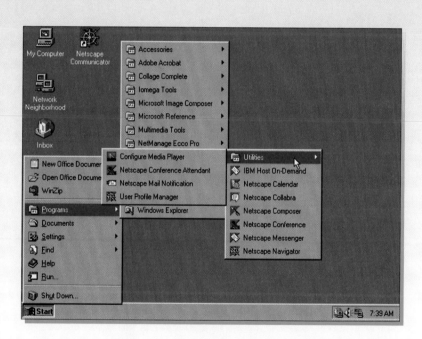

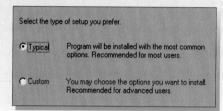

4 The Setup Type dialog box offers you three setup choices. Choose Typical by clicking the top button.

5 Communicator's installation program will automatically suggest a place where Communicator should be installed: on your hard drive in Program Files with your other software programs. Click Next to accept and continue.

6 Communicator's installation program will also automatically suggest a program folder name: Netscape Communicator. Click Next to accept and continue.

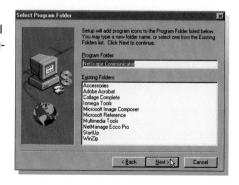

How to Create a New User Profile

After you have installed Communicator from either the Internet or from a CD-ROM, you will be asked to create a user profile. You must create one profile to use Communicator, and it is a good idea to go back and create others if more than one person will be using the program. This exercise outlines the basic steps for first-time setup, and in the FYI section you will find instructions on how to create more user profiles after Communicator has been installed.

1 After you've installed Communicator, the User Profile Manager will ask you to create a new User Profile. Click the New button once to get started.

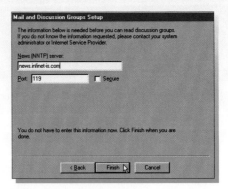

6 Finally, enter the name of your news server and click Finish when you're done. This completes your new profile setup, and Communicator will automatically launch itself so you can get to work.

● If you want to create more User Profiles after you've installed Communicator, exit the program or do the following steps before you launch it: Click once on the Windows' Start button in the lower left corner of the screen, then choose Programs, then Netscape Communicator, then Utilities, then User Profile Manager. Click the New button once to create a new profile.

● Remember that each time you create a new User Profile, you will have to reset or reestablish Preferences and other customizable settings. This is both the benefit and the drawback of different User Profiles.

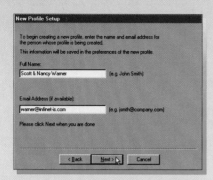

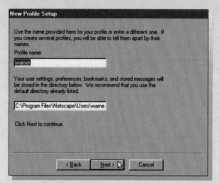

2 Read the introductory information and click Next to move on. Now the Manager will ask for your full name and user (e-mail) address. Type in this information and click Next.

3 The Profile Manager will automatically assign you a user name based on the first portion of your e-mail address and it will establish a storage area on your computer for all the e-mail, files, newsgroup postings, and other information that you download from the Internet while using Communicator. Click Next to accept these settings.

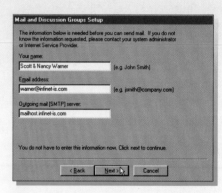

4 Now the Manager will ask for the name of your outgoing SMTP mail server—this is information that your Internet service provider should give you when you establish your e-mail account. Type in the server address and click Next to continue.

5 Now give the Manager the name of your incoming mail server, and click Next to continue. You must provide Communicator with these correct server addresses or you will not be able to use Messenger and/or Collabra for e-mail or newsgroup postings.

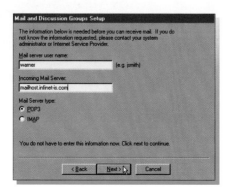

How to Register Netscape Communicator

Now that you've successfully installed Communicator on your desktop PC, you're going to register Communicator with Netscape before you begin exploring. Registration is a two-step process. First you'll enter your user information, which includes your name, address, and other information that Netscape will use to establish your registration. Then you'll participate in a short survey about what you use Communicator for, what kind of business you're in, and more.

1 After you've successfully installed Netscape Communicator and signed up with an Internet service provider (ISP), you'll want to register with Netscape. Registration will enable you to receive better technical support and early notice of Netscape upgrades.

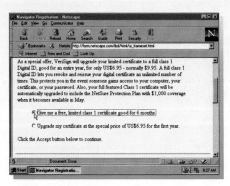

6 Now you must register for your Digital Certificate, which is another unique identification to help you on the Internet. Read through the description if you have time; otherwise, choose the free limited certificate by clicking the first option. Now read the subscriber agreement and click Accept.

(Continued on next page)

● Previous versions of Netscape Navigator have required you to register the name of your Internet service provider (ISP), some basic information about your modem, and other basics of your computer setup. You'll still need to set your modem and your Internet account separately, even though Netscape doesn't require you to provide this information when you register.

2 To reach the Registration area, log on to the Internet and launch Navigator. Place your cursor on the Help pull-down menu along the top of Navigator's window, click once, and scroll down till you reach Register Now. Click once.

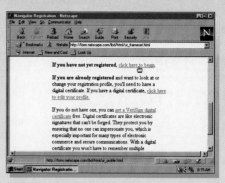

3 You're going to give Netscape some basic information about yourself and your computer setup in this first step of the registration process. There's a line of text that reads "If you have not yet registered, click here to begin." Click the underlined portion once to proceed.

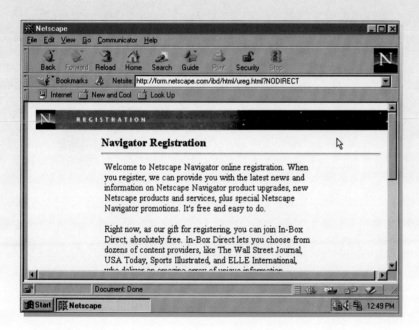

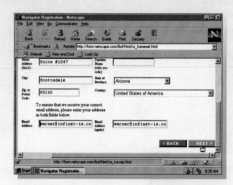

4 In this screen, enter your name, address, and other information (if it's marked with a red asterisk, you must supply the information requested). Be sure to type in your e-mail address twice; Netscape needs this for verification. Click Next when you're done, then click Continue. (You'll explore Netscape's Security measures in Part 7.)

5 Now you'll be asked to answer simple questions about where, how, and why you use Communicator. Click the arrows to the left of the answer blanks to choose from the pull-down menus. Then click OK when you're done, then click Continue.

How to Register Netscape Communicator
(Continued)

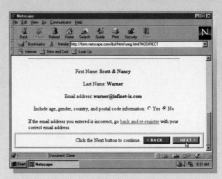

7 Verify that DigiSign has your name and e-mail address confirmed correctly, decide if you want them to have your other information (age, gender, and so forth), then click Next when you're finished. A new window will appear informing you that Communicator is about to generate your Private Key. Click OK to continue.

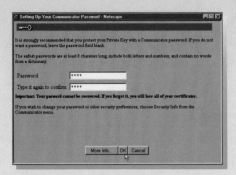

8 Now Communicator will ask you for a password. Choose something you will remember but something that no one else can guess—you can never ask DigiSign for your password if you forget it, so choose carefully. Click OK to continue.

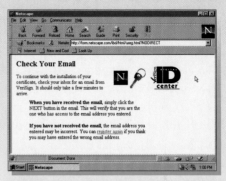

9 DigiSign will send you an e-mail message to verify that your Private Key has been issued. Wait a few moments, then check your e-mail to make sure you've received it. Then simply click OK in your message, and your personal certificate registration is all finished.

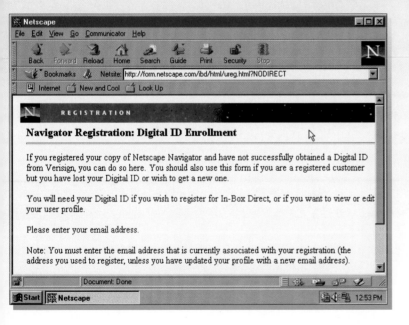

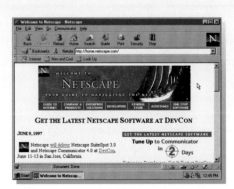

10 Your registration with Netscape is now complete. Click the Back button to return to Netscape's home page, or continue on with the next lesson in this Part.

How to Get Technical Support from Netscape

Everybody needs a little help sometimes when it comes to learning a new software program, from the most experienced Web surfer to the "newbie," or brand-new first-time Web user. Netscape Communicator 4 not only offers an entire Help menu (which will be covered in more detail later in the book) but many other ways to get technical assistance and general support for all parts of Netscape Communicator, including Navigator.

① As already mentioned, there's a Help pull-down menu located at the top of the Communicator window. For now, choose Product Information and Support. You'll explore this menu more thoroughly later on in this part of the book.

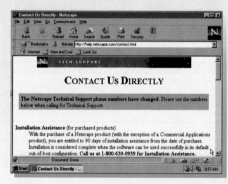

⑦ If you just can't find what you're looking for, or you want to talk to a real live Netscape expert, How To Get Help provides you with phone numbers, e-mail addresses, and other ways to reach help.

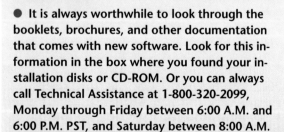

FYI

● It is always worthwhile to look through the booklets, brochures, and other documentation that comes with new software. Look for this information in the box where you found your installation disks or CD-ROM. Or you can always call Technical Assistance at 1-800-320-2099, Monday through Friday between 6:00 A.M. and 6:00 P.M. PST, and Saturday between 8:00 A.M. and 4:00 P.M. PST.

● If you're looking at the green Netscape toolbar on Netscape's home page, you don't necessarily want to click on the Assistance button. This is an area where nontechnical questions about Netscape products and services are answered, though there is also a link to Technical Support.

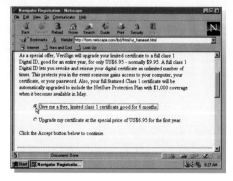

⑥ Info Search allows you to access and use a searchable information database. You answer some simple questions and the database offers some suggestions.

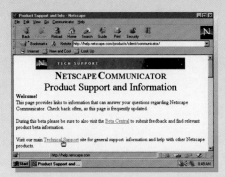

2 Welcome to the Product Support and Information area of Netscape's home page. This is the place to visit and find answers to any questions you might have. For now, click the link that reads Technical Support once.

3 Now look at the green toolbar, or row of buttons, just beneath the Technical Support logo. The Newcomer's Guide is the button to click if you're a first-time Web surfer. Netscape provides you with an easy-to-read and -understand way to find what you need, from a troubleshooting guide to a database of answers

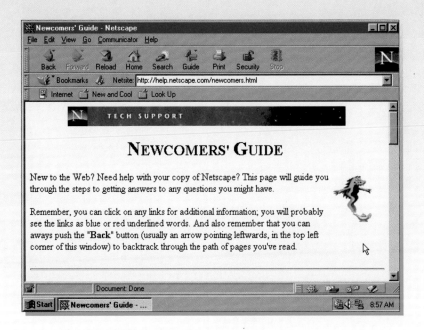

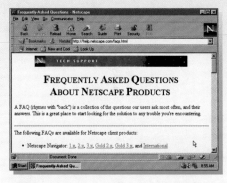

4 The Frequently Asked Questions page or "FAQ" (rhymes with "back") is a list of common questions and their corresponding answers. Just what you need when all you want are the "FAQs."

5 Ask Mozilla is where you meet Netscape's dragon mascot, and where you can find answers by using the same techniques and information used by Netscape's senior support team.

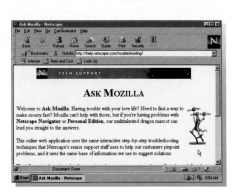

How to Use Navigator's Main Toolbar

A s you know, Communicator is a pretty easy application to install and set up; and the tools you'll use to surf the Web with Communicator are also easy to use. When you first launch Communicator after you've signed on with an Internet service provider, you'll be directed to the Netscape home page. It just so happens that Netscape's home page is the default home page for their product; later on, you'll learn how to set a different home page as your default. Along the top of Communicator's display window, you'll see a toolbar with nine tool buttons: Back, Forward, Reload, Home, Search, Guide, Print, Security, and Stop.

1 The first two toolbar buttons will help you move from page to page when you've been surfing around a while. The first one, the Back button, returns you to the last Web page you visited. The Forward button helps you out if you've skipped back and you want to go forward again.

● If you forget what an item on the toolbar does (and you might, because they're not labeled) you can simply place the cursor over the top of the button you want to identify. Almost immediately, a bubble will pop open with a short description of the tool's function, and at the same time, a second description will appear in the message box along the bottom left of Communicator's window. So Communicator gives you two nearly instant ways to remind yourself what each item on the toolbar stands for.

● A new feature in Communicator allows you to switch the positions of the button bars. Move your mouse pointer to the tiny open/close tabs on the left side of the two button bars. The arrow-shaped cursor becomes a hand, and you can click and drag each button bar to switch its position.

8 The Stop button stops the loading of a Web page in progress and is only displayed while you're waiting for a new page to appear.

7 The Security button is part of Navigator's improved security capabilities—here, it's "unlocked," which means it's inactive. You'll learn more about this topic in Part 7.

2 The Reload button reloads the page you want if, for example, it's missing a graphic or some of the text is garbled.

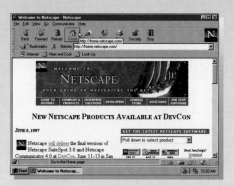

3 The Home button takes you back to the very beginning—in this case, the Netscape home page.

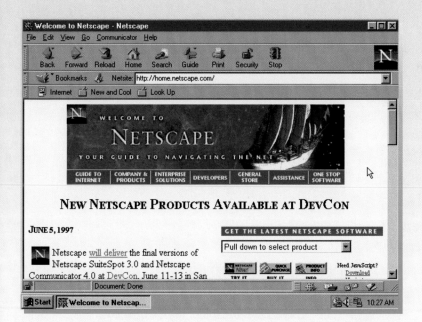

4 The Search button links you to another part of Netscape's Web site where you can begin a general keyword search on any subject using a *search engine*. You'll learn more about searching and surfing the Web in Part 2.

6 The Print button enables you to print a paper copy of the Web page displayed on your screen.

5 The Guide button directs you to one of five locations: The Internet for starting a keyword search with Yahoo!; the People page where you can search for a person's e-mail address; the Yellow Pages for finding a business' street and Web addresses; the What's New list of, well, what's new; and the What's Cool list of Netscape's most interesting links.

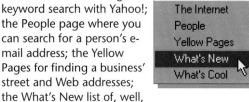

How to Use Navigator's Other Tools

If you upgraded your Netscape Navigator from version 3, you've probably already noticed that the Directory buttons are gone. In their place are a handful of new buttons on the top and bottom of the Navigator window. The second group of buttons are, in clockwise order, the Bookmark QuickFile button, the Quick Link button, the familiar N Netscape button, and the Composition toolbar, which holds five buttons: the Navigator button, the Mailbox button, the Discussions button, the Composer button, and the Show/Dock button.

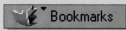

1 The Bookmark Quick File button is a shortcut you'll use to add and delete bookmarks. You'll learn more about Navigator's Bookmark capabilities in Part 2.

8 Finally, if you roll the cursor over the inconspicuous "X" button at the top of the Component toolbar, it jumps to the lower right corner of Navigator's window. Click the tab (now with a tiny open/close tab on the left side) once more to restore it to its original position.

7 The Composer button opens Netscape Composer, Netscape's HTML or Web page editor, formerly known as Navigator Gold. You'll learn more about Netscape Composer in Part 6.

2 The Quick Link button also allows you to quickly add a new bookmark by clicking and dragging it to the Bookmark Quick File button—which, again, is discussed in detail in Part 2.

3 The big N or Netscape button will always return you to Netscape's home page, even if you change your default home page by customizing the Home button. (There's more about this later in this part of the book.)

4 Now look at the floating, rectangular Component bar to the right of Communicator's open window. There are four buttons on it; the first is the Navigator button, which opens a new browser window also in Navigator, if you want to open another Web site separately.

5 The Mailbox button is your e-mail inbox where you can read, write, and manage your e-mail with Netscape Messenger. You'll learn more about Netscape Messenger in Part 3.

6 The Discussions button links you to Netscape Collabra, the newsgroup reader, which enables you to browse newsgroup posts. You'll learn more about Netscape Collabra in Part 4.

How to Use Navigator's File Pull-Down Menu

Once you become familiar and comfortable with Navigator's pull-down menus, you'll use them all the time. In this section you'll explore each of Navigator's File menu capabilities, which have been greatly extended compared to what was available in previous versions of Netscape. Not only does the File menu give you fast and easy ways to open new browser windows and print interesting Web pages, but it also gives you shortcut access to Netscape Messenger and Netscape Composer, the e-mail management and HTML editing tools included with Communicator 4.

1 Begin by opening the File pull-down menu—click once on the word "file" near the upper left corner of Navigator's window. This is how you open all of Navigator's pull-down menus.

7 The Close command closes the Navigator window without exiting Navigator, and Exit shuts down the program when you're finished.

6 Page Setup allows you to change margins, and to work with headers and footers and other features of an open document. Print Preview shows you what a page will look like on paper before you print it. Print lets you print exactly what you see in the *active* or currently open window.

● As you open the pull-down menus and explore the tools, you'll notice shortcut keyboard commands listed to the right of each menu item. You use these shortcuts by holding down the Control (Ctrl) key and a letter or function key at the same time. Consult the inside of the back cover for a list of Communicator's keyboard shortcuts.

2 Choosing New will open a sub-menu which allows you to open (in descending order) a new Navigator window for browsing (Navigator Window); a new window for composing e-mail with Messenger (Message); and/or a new Web page with Blank Page, Page from Template, or a Page from Wizard in Composer. Open Page opens a Web page already in progress.

3 Save As lets you save and name an open document, while Save Frame As will become useful later on after you learn more about frames in general.

4 The Send Page item allows you to use e-mail to send a Web page to another person; Edit Page lets you make changes to an open Web page; Edit Frame is another intermediate feature you'll learn more about in future chapters; and Upload File lets you *upload* or send a file to an FTP site.

5 Go Offline lets you read e-mail and newsgroup posts when you're not connected to the Internet.

How to Use Navigator's Edit Pull-Down Menu

Now that you've had a good introduction to pull-down menus, let's move on to the other five menus listed along the top of Navigator's window. The Edit menu, which is what you'll explore in this part of the chapter, will become very useful to you as you eventually surf around the World Wide Web. It's also the place where you access your Preferences files when you are ready to customize Navigator.

1 Begin by opening the Edit pull-down menu just as you opened the File pull-down menu in the last section.

6 The Preferences submenu at the very end of the Edit menu is what you'll use to personalize Navigator later on in this part of the book.

● As you open the pull-down menus and explore the tools, you'll notice abbreviated shortcut keyboard commands listed to the right of each menu item. You use these shortcuts by holding down the Control (Ctrl) key and a letter or function key at the same time. Consult the inside of the back cover for a list of all Communicator's keyboard shortcuts.

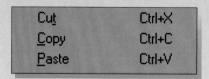

2 Cut, Copy, and Paste are for cutting (removing), copying (duplicating), and pasting (inserting) sections of a Web page you want to rearrange or keep.

3 Select All enables you to rearrange, save, or delete all items on a Web page.

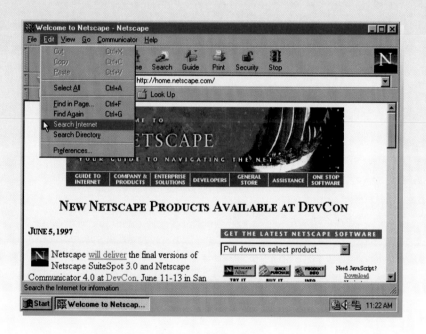

| Find in Page... | Ctrl+F |
| Find Again | Ctrl+G |

4 Find In Page and Find Again allow you to find a certain word or phrase on a Web page without manually scrolling up and down using the slider bar—the button between the arrows on the right side of Navigator's window. You move it by clicking and dragging it.

5 Search Internet initiates a Web-site keyword search while Search Directory looks for a name, e-mail address, or phone number (both of these kinds of searches are covered thoroughly in Part 2).

Search Internet
Search Directory

How to Use Navigator's View Pull-Down Menu

You'll probably use Navigator's pull-down menus as often as you surf the Web, as each menu contains essential commands for easy navigation. In each of the pull-down menus, most features have unique keyboard commands. Some users will find that once they learn the keyboard commands, they can work faster by keeping their fingers on the keyboard, rather than pointing, dragging, and clicking with the mouse. However, surfing the Web is pretty mouse-intensive, and it might be just as easy to use the pull-down menus. You'll learn about both, so you can use the method that works best for you.

1 Begin by opening the View pull-down menu—click View once to leave it open.

Encoding ▶

8 Encoding is a foreign language customization capability that you don't have to think about. If you're using this book, you're reading English, so the Western default setting is exactly what you need.

Page Services

7 Page Services is an advanced feature strictly for use by systems and network administrators.

FYI

● As you open the pull-down menus and explore the tools, you'll notice shortcut keyboard commands listed to the right of each menu item. You use these shortcuts by holding down the Control (Ctrl) key and a letter or function key at the same time. Consult the inside of the back cover for a list of Communicator's keyboard shortcuts.

Hide <u>N</u>avigation Toolbar
Show <u>L</u>ocation Toolbar
Hide <u>P</u>ersonal Toolbar

2 Show/Hide Navigation Toolbar, Show/Hide Location Toolbar, and Show/Hide Personal Toolbar alternatively conceal and bring back each of Navigator's toolbars.

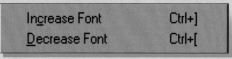

In<u>c</u>rease Font   Ctrl+]
<u>D</u>ecrease Font   Ctrl+[

3 Increase Font and Decrease Font enlarge or reduce the font size of the pages displayed by Navigator for easier reading and/or fitting more text in the window.

<u>R</u>eload   Ctrl+R
Sho<u>w</u> Images
Re<u>f</u>resh

4 Reload works like the Reload button on the main toolbar: it downloads the current Web page again. Show Images downloads a Web page's pictures if you have Auto Load Images disabled, and Refresh updates a Web page by comparing the version on your screen to the version on the Web and showing you which is most current.

Page So<u>u</u>rce   Ctrl+U
Page <u>I</u>nfo   Ctrl+I

6 Page Source and Page Info are features you may use later on when you begin building your own Web pages in Part 6 and when we discuss security in Part 7.

<u>S</u>top Page Loading   <Esc>
Stop <u>A</u>nimations

5 Stop Page Loading is like the Stop button on the main toolbar—it interrupts a page in mid-download—and Stop Animations pauses any animations on a Web page you're viewing.

How to Use Navigator's Go Pull-Down Menu

Besides File, Edit, and View, another useful pull-down menu is Go, although you may eventually prefer using toolbar tools to do many of the functions displayed here. However, there are some unique features to the Go menu along with the basic navigational controls. With the Go menu, you can go back, forward, and home. You can establish a link directly to the location of your own Web site (once you build one; we'll introduce you to Netscape Composer in Part 6). You can also stop loading a Web page while it's in progress, and you can view a history list that records which Web sites you have visited.

1 Open the Go pull-down menu and click the mouse button once to keep the menu open.

The Weather Channel - Home Page
1
2 The Internet Movie Database
✓ 3 The New York Times on the Web
4 Quicken Financial Network
5 Fodor's Travel Online
6 ESPN SportsZone: S..., statistics and more
7 Outside Online
8 PC Magazine Online
9 Welcome to Netscape
Yahoo!

Welcome to Netscape
Tech Support
Product Support and Info

5 The rest of the Go menu is a list of all the sites you've visited during your current Web surfing session. A checkmark appears to the left of the name of the Web page you're currently visiting, and all the individual pages are numbered according to the order you visited them in.

FYI

● As you open the pull-down menus and explore the tools, you'll notice shortcut keyboard commands listed to the right of each menu item. You use these shortcuts by holding down the Control (Ctrl) key and a letter or function key at the same time. Consult the inside of the back cover for a list of Communicator's keyboard shortcuts.

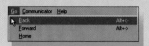

2 Back works the same as the Back button on the main toolbar—use it to move backward to Web pages you've already visited.

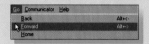

3 Forward, also the same as the Forward button on the main toolbar, takes you to the most current page after you've used the Back button.

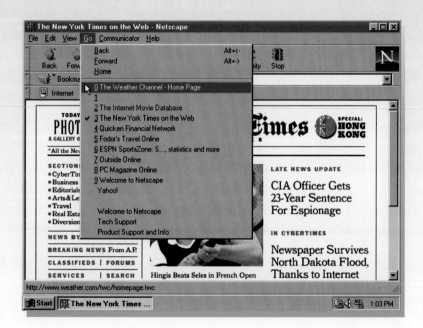

4 Home, like the Home button on the main toolbar, will always take you to your default home page—this is a preference you'll establish in the next part.

How to Use Navigator's Communicator Pull-Down Menu

By using the Communicator menu, you can access all of Communicator's capabilities quickly and easily—you can get to your e-mail, you can begin building a Web page, you can join a newsgroup discussion, and you can find information in your address book or bookmarks file—and much more.

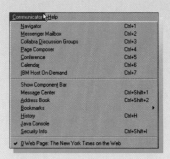

1 To open the Communicator pull-down menu, move the cursor to the word Communicator at the top of Navigator's window. Click once and the menu will open.

9 Finally, at the bottom of the Window menu there is a list of all the Web pages you've visited during your current session, numbered in chronological order. Here, you've only been one place so you only have one location listed.

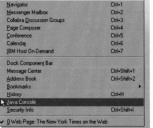

8 Java Console is an advanced Web page building feature you may use if you become an advanced Web page designer.

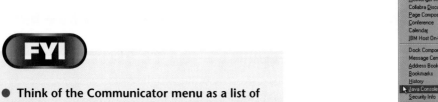

FYI

● Think of the Communicator menu as a list of shortcuts to all the aspects of Netscape Communicator: Netscape Messenger for e-mail, Netscape Collabra for newsgroups, Netscape Composer for constructing Web pages, plus some handy features of Netscape Navigator, the Web browser.

2 Navigator opens a new Navigator window; Messenger Mailbox opens your e-mail; Collabra Discussions Groups opens your newsgroup postings; Page Composer opens a blank Web page; and Conference launches Communicator's long-distance calling program (there's more on these other components in Parts 3, 4, 5, and 6, respectively).

3 Show/Dock Component Bar determines the location of the button bar in the lower right corner of Navigator's window—in the center figure in this section, it's "docked," but here it's "shown."

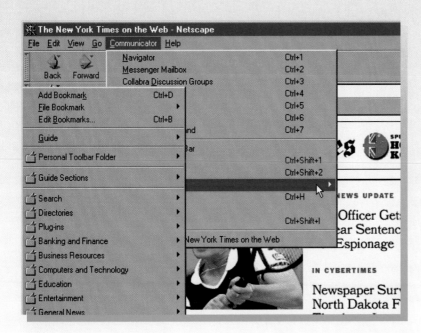

4 Message Center opens your e-mail and newsgroups message center, which will be explained more thoroughly in Parts 3 and 4.

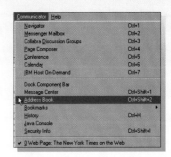

5 Address Book will be a list of e-mail addresses and newsgroups you write to frequently—you'll establish it in Part 3.

7 History is a detailed, more technical list of all the sites you've visited during your current session. For now, you may feel satisfied with the list at the end of this menu, which is close to the same thing.

6 Bookmarks is a way to memorize and keep the URLs or addresses of Web pages you want to visit many times. You'll begin building your bookmark file in Part 2.

How to Use Navigator's Help Menu

The Help menu is one of Navigator's best features for the new user. You may remember using some of these features earlier to register your Netscape Communicator software with Netscape, and to get technical support. This section explores all the Help menu items in greater detail.

1 To open the Help pull-down menu, move the cursor to the word Help at the top of Navigator's window. Click once and the menu will open.

8 About Communicator, the last item on the Help menu, is some legal jargon that you may or may not want to read. Either way, you've finished looking at the Help menu and the entire set of pull-down menus. Now you're on your way.

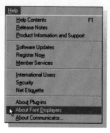

7 About Font Displayers touches on questions concerning dynamic text and other, similar subjects.

● As you open the pull-down menus and explore the tools, you'll notice shortcut keyboard commands listed to the right of each menu item. You use these shortcuts by holding down the Control (Ctrl) key and a letter or function key at the same time. Consult the inside of the back cover for a list of Communicator's keyboard shortcuts.

Help Contents   F1
Release Notes
Product Information and Support

2 If you want to read about Navigator's various features and capabilities, you would click Help Contents, Release Notes, and/or Product Information and Support. We will explore how to use Help Contents, or NetHelp, in one of the Projects at the end of the book.

Software Updates
Register Now
Member Services

3 We've already checked out Software Updates and Register Now earlier in Part 1, and Member Services contains the same type of information.

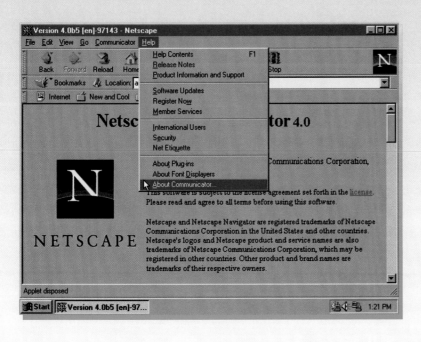

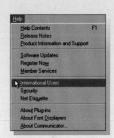

4 International Members contains specific information about using Communicator with languages other than English, and in countries outside the United States.

Security
Net Etiquette

5 Security is covered in depth in Part 7 along with other security issues, and Net Etiquette provides newcomers to the Internet with an outline of basic online manners.

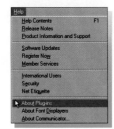

6 About Plug-ins is a list of audio, video, and other multimedia components already installed on your computer with Communicator.

How to Use Navigator's Help Menu: Extending Navigator's Setup

You've already registered Netscape Communicator—the entire suite of Netscape products included in version 4 along with Navigator—so you're ready to surf, to send e-mail, to join a newsgroup, to build a Web page, and more. Now you have the option to explore Navigator's extended capabilities, and the option to choose what you may want to add on.

The Software option on the Help pull-down menu brings you to a part of Netscape's Web site where you can read about and purchase Netscape software upgrades, sign up for a personal certificate (a password replacement), "supercharge" Navigator with additional components, and more.

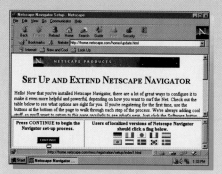

1 To get started, access the Navigator extension page by choosing Software from the Help pull-down menu. You'll arrive at a split screen made up of two frames. Click the Next button near the bottom left corner of the screen.

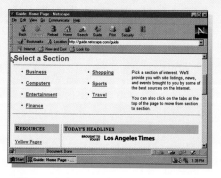

6 You've just finished the extended registration setup, so you're ready to continue your exploration of Navigator, or begin surfing the Web.

● You can purchase Netscape Communicator or other Netscape software and download software upgrades from this page as well. Use the slider bar to find more information in the top frame of the main registration extension page.

2 If you've already registered Netscape Communicator (described earlier) you'll see the words 1) Registration in bold print along the bottom of the window. You want to explore the last three steps, so click the Continue button near the bottom right corner of the window.

3 Now you've reached the Components page. Use the slider button along the right side of the Navigator window to scroll down and read about standard and additional Navigator plug-ins and helper applications. You'll also find more on these options in Part 7. Click Continue to proceed.

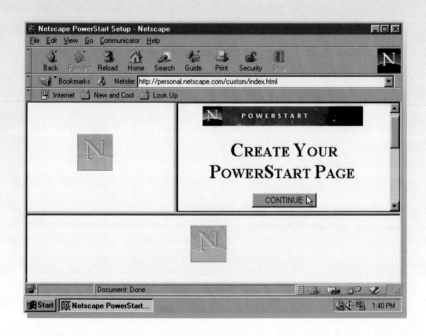

4 The Digital Passport page is an introduction to a Navigator encryption feature, the personal certificate. Click Continue to proceed.

5 The last part of the registration extension page offers you three suggestions on where to begin surfing the Web via Netscape's Web site: Destinations, a list of business-related Web sites; PowerStart, a way to customize Web page display; and the Netscape General Store.

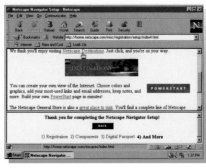

How to Set Appearance Preferences: Fonts and Colors

O f all the preferences you'll set, your Appearance Preferences will affect your everyday surfing experiences the most. Through the Appearance Preferences menu, you can set your own default home page; you can customize fonts, colors, and the appearance of links; and more.

1 After you've launched Communicator, choose Preferences from the Edit menu and click once. You'll see the complete Preferences menu, along with a category listing along the left side; click once on all the plus (+) symbols to "open" these sub-menus so you can see what they contain.

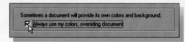

6 Finally, decide if you want to automatically override an incoming Web page's color choices with your own (you don't). So leave this setting as it is, too, and let's move on to set the rest of your Preferences.

● Don't go overboard with changing fonts, styles, and colors, or you may change the appearance of Web pages too much. Remember that most of the Web sites you'll find have been designed with your computer's default preferences in mind.

2 Click once on Appearance in the category listing. This is where you decide which component(s) should automatically open when you launch Communicator—you can choose up to all six of Communicator's individual components. For now, simply leave Navigator checked.

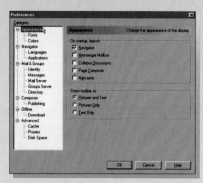

3 The bottom portion of the Appearance submenu lets you decide if you want Navigator's Toolbar buttons to display as pictures and text, just pictures, or just text. It would be best to leave this setting as it is until you are very familiar with the Toolbar buttons, so leave things as they are. Click the Fonts submenu category listing to proceed.

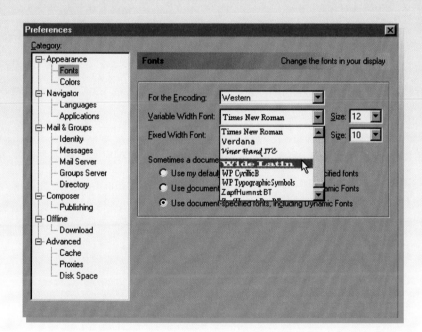

4 Fonts gives you a visual example of how various kinds of text will be displayed by Communicator. This is also where you decide if and when you want your customized font choices to override fonts in an incoming Web page (you don't). Choose your settings, then click the Colors category listing once.

5 The Colors submenu enables you to choose customized colors for links, page text, and other online features. You can also decide if you want Navigator to underline links (you do). Make your choices and click the Navigator category listing once.

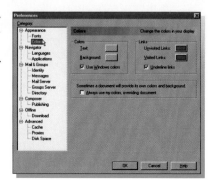

How to Set Navigator Preferences: Languages and Applications

Now that you've learned how to customize the basic look of the Web pages you'll view, you can learn how to customize how Web pages behave. In this part, you can decide when and how Web page images will appear, what supporting and helper applications you want to use, and what foreign languages you want to be able to view (if any). Most likely, you'll want to leave these Preferences settings exactly as they are for now. Once you become much more familiar with Navigator, Composer, and others parts of Communicator, you may want to come back.

1 Open the Edit pull-down menu and choose Preferences. Now choose the Navigator category submenu and click it once.

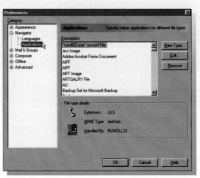

5 Applications is a complete list of all the helper applications Communicator uses to read all the kinds of files you may find or download while you're on the Internet. This is a list of settings you should not change until (or unless) you become extremely Web-savvy, so let's move on to the next set of Preferences.

● Try not to feel overwhelmed with all the choices you're given in the Preferences menu. These exercises are designed as an introduction, not a technical manual. So if you don't understand what a particular setting is for, just go on to the next one. Some of Navigator's features and options are designed for advanced users only, and becoming advanced takes time and experience.

2 The Navigator submenu is where you can change the default home page to something other than Netscape's home page. Change it now to **http://www.zdnet.com/~pccomp**, PC Computing magazine's home page.

3 You can also decide how long you want Communicator to remember, or *cache*, the Web sites you've visited. Later on, when you become a more experienced surfer, you may want to reduce this amount of saving time because you can build up too much memory. But for now, leave the default setting as it is at nine days and click the Languages category submenu once.

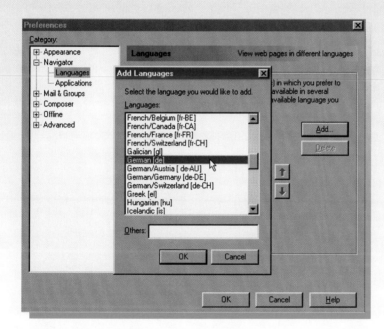

4 Languages is a special Preferences menu that enables Communicator to display Web pages written in languages other than English in their native alphabets using diacritical marks, non-Roman alphabets, and so on. You can leave these settings alone, and click the Applications category submenu listing to move on.

How to Set Mail and Groups Preferences: Preparing for E-Mail and Newsgroup Postings

Without configuring your e-mail address, mail server, and news server, you can't send or receive e-mail or subscribe to newsgroups. Setting these preferences is probably something you'll only have to do once, but you'll want to keep this information in mind for future reference—for instance, if you change Internet service providers or if you want to disable newsgroup subscription.

1 Open the Edit pull-down menu and choose Preferences. Now choose the Mail & Groups category submenu and click it once.

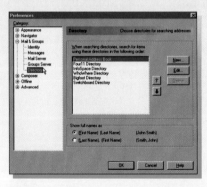

6 Directory is a Preferences submenu you may wish to customize again after learning how to use White and Yellow pages in Part 2: this submenu enables you to list different directories in order of preference so that Communicator will automatically search your favorites directories first. For now, leave the default list in place and we'll move on to other Preferences.

● Try not to feel overwhelmed with all the choices you're given in the Preferences menu. These exercises are designed as an introduction, not a technical manual. So if you don't understand what a particular setting is for, just go on to the next one. Some of Navigator's features and options are designed for advanced users only, and becoming advanced takes time and experience.

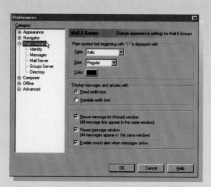

2 Mail & Groups enables you to customize the appearance of quoted text, messages, and articles. This is also where you decide if you want Communicator to "beep" you when new messages arrive if you have Messenger and/or Collabra running; for now, leave the enable sound alert option off. Click the Identity submenu category to continue.

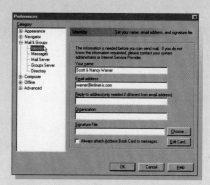

3 Identity is the extremely important Preferences area where you establish your name, e-mail address, a different return address, and other necessary information. You can also change your Address Book Card, something you'll explore in greater detail in Part 3. You cannot send e-mail or newsgroup postings without filling these blanks in, so do so and click Messages to continue.

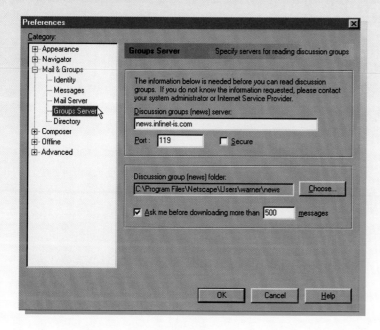

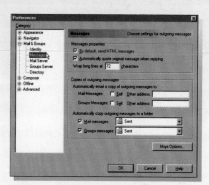

4 Messages is the place where you decide if you want to save copies of every e-mail and/or newsgroup posting you send, and where you save them. Make your choices and then click the Mail Server category submenu to continue.

5 Mail Server and Groups Server require you to type in information you need to get from your Internet service provider. If you do not know your ingoing and outgoing SMTP mail server name or your news NNTP server name, contact your ISP. You cannot send or receive e-mail or newsgroup postings without providing Communicator with this information. Click Directory category submenu to continue.

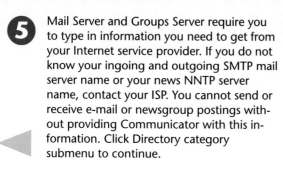

How to Set Composer Preferences: Web Site Publishing

For the most part, your Composer Preferences will not affect your Communicator experience until you begin building your own Web pages in Part 6. Then you'll want to return to this group of submenus and establish where and how you'll create Web pages; to decide on a customized set of color and background defaults; and to set some basic publishing controls to protect your work.

1 Open the Edit pull-down menu and choose Preferences. Now choose the Composer category submenu and click it once.

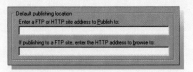

5 The default publishing location Preference settings, on the lower half of this Preferences submenu, will enable you to save Web page files directly to an FTP site later on if you prefer. For now, leave these address spaces empty, though, and let's proceed toward the next group of Preferences.

● Try not to feel overwhelmed with all the choices you're given in the Preferences menu. These exercises are designed as an introduction, not a technical manual. So if you don't understand what a particular setting is for, just go on to the next one. Some of Navigator's features and options are designed for advanced users only, and becoming advanced takes time and experience.

2 The Composer category submenu first enables you to list yourself as the author of all Web pages you construct with Netscape Composer, which is information other Web page authors will be able to find once you display your pages on the Internet. This is also the place where you establish how often you want Composer to save your Web pages as you are building them. The default setting is ten minutes, but you may want to decrease this setting as you get faster with Composer; you can create, and lose, a lot of work in ten minutes.

3 Next on this page, if you're already proficient in building Web pages, here's the place you list your other Web page editor program (such as netObjects Fusion or BBEdit) and an image editor like Adobe Photoshop or Adobe Illustrator. This is also where you can make some relative font size decisions, but only in the future if this becomes a concern. For now, click the Publishing category submenu listing and we'll move on.

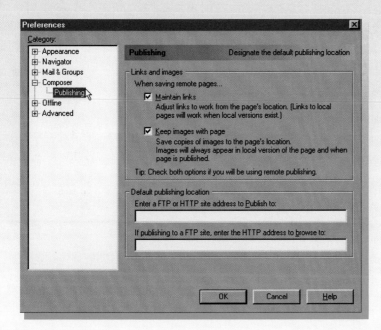

4 These Preferences settings are intermediate-level Web publishing settings that you should not disturb until (or if) you become extremely proficient in building Web pages. The top half of this Preferences submenu involves where and how to save Web pages and their related images. As mentioned, leave the default setting where it is for now.

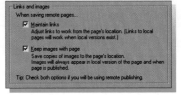

How to Set Offline Preferences: Communicator, Mail, and Newsgroups

After you become adept at managing your e-mail and newsgroup postings, you may prefer to read and respond to them offline—that is, when you are not connected to your Internet service provider. Why would you want to do this? To save yourself money if your ISP charges you by the hour after a certain length of time; to free your phone line if your computer and telephone are in competition; for many good and/or economical reasons.

1 Open the Edit pull-down menu and choose Preferences. Now choose the Offline category sub-menu and click it once.

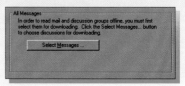

5 Finally, the All Messages preference setting is something you'll establish later on in Part 4 when you get set to read newsgroups with Netscape Collabra. Plan on coming back to this place later, and let's set up the last group of Preferences.

● Try not to feel overwhelmed with all the choices you're given in the Preferences menu. These exercises are designed as an introduction, not a technical manual. So if you don't understand what a particular setting is for, just go on to the next one. Some of Navigator's features and options are designed for advanced users only, and becoming advanced takes time and experience.

2 This submenu presents you with three choices for deciding how you want to work with Communicator, and here they are in English: choose the first option (Online Work Mode) if you are using Communicator at work on a network and you leave it running all day long.

3 However, if you are using Communicator at home in your spare time, or in any other situation where you're not on a network, choose the second option (Offline Work Mode). If you're using Communicator on a laptop in different situations or if neither of the first two options seem applicable, choose the third option (Ask Me). For now, assume you're using Communicator only a few hours a day and choose Option Number Two. Then click the Download category submenu listing once and we'll move on.

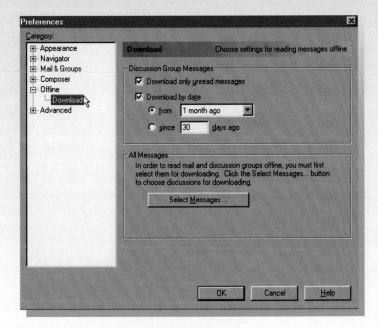

4 The Discussion Group Messages preference setting at the top of the Download submenu is another potential time and money saver: You definitely want to limit the number of newsgroup postings either by number, date, or whether or not you've read them. Otherwise you could spend a small fortune downloading messages you don't want.

How to Set Advanced Preferences: Cache Size, Disk Space, and More

At the beginning of this book, you were told you would come across various features and aspects of Communicator that were strictly advanced and not at all for newcomers. The Advanced Preferences section of your general preferences definitely fall in this category—here you'll be briefly introduced to various parts of Communicator that you may someday want to change, but are most likely better left seen but untouched for the moment.

1 Open the Edit pull-down menu and choose Preferences. Now choose the Advanced category submenu listing and click it once.

8 Now you're absolutely finished establishing all your preferences, so click OK to save any changes you made. This saves your settings and wraps up this last section of Part 1.

FYI

● Try not to feel overwhelmed with all the choices you're given in the Preferences menu. These exercises are designed as an introduction, not a technical manual. So if you don't understand what a particular setting is for, just go on to the next one. Some of Navigator's features and options are designed for advanced users only, and becoming advanced takes time and experience.

7 ...while the Discussion Groups Messages Only preferences let you decide how many and/or what kind of newsgroup postings you want to keep.

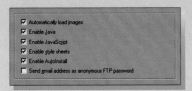

2 The first group of preferences affect many online technologies (such as Java, JavaScript, and style sheets) that spice up many cool Web sites. If you uncheck these boxes, you will disable these features and miss something you might want to see. (The exception to this is the box already left unchecked—you may or may not have the chance to visit an FTP site, so leave this preference alone.)

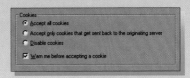

3 The bottom half of this preference submenu deals with *cookies*, a new kind of program or software response many advertising and marketing-oriented sites use to record your visit. If this idea bothers you (and it does bother some people) here's where you can choose to be warned, so you can accept or refuse cookies at your discretion, or to disable all cookies all the time. It's your call; make it and click the Cache submenu category listing to continue.

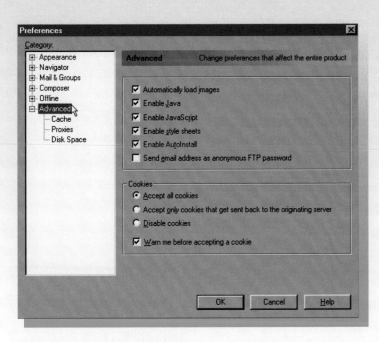

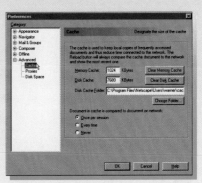

4 Communicator's *caches* are where Web pages are temporarily stored on your computer so you can use the Back and Forward Toolbar buttons, as an example, to move among Web sites you've recently visited. This is where you decide how large these caches should be, and how often Communicator should reload a Web page to update it. For now, leave these settings as they are and click the Proxies submenu category listing.

6 The Disk Space preferences help you manage the size of your e-mail messages and newsgroup postings, especially if you decided to keep copies of your outgoing correspondence earlier in the Messages/Mail & Groups submenu. The All Messages preferences enable Communicator to screen and/or compact extremely large e-mail messages to save on space…

5 The Proxies preference submenu is only important to you if you are using Communicator behind a firewall, an extra measure of security used by many corporations and businesses that can prevent Internet users inside from doing certain tasks. If you're using Communicator on your own computer at home, this isn't an issue. So leave the setting as it is and click the Disk Space submenu category listing to proceed.

PART 2

Catching Your First Wave: Start Exploring the Web

SO FAR, you've successfully installed and set up Communicator and learned to use most of Navigator's basic tools. Up until this point, your surfing has been pretty limited; you've looked around the Netscape home page and changed your default home page to the PC Computing Web site. However, in keeping with the surfing metaphor, there are always bigger and better waves out there if you have the time and know where to look.

IN THIS SECTION YOU'LL LEARN

How to Surf: Some Basic Tips and Tricks

Here's your basic, no-frills introduction to surfing the World Wide Web—no assumptions, no nonsense, and no rules. Navigating the Web means working with *links*, or connections between individual Web pages, and the Web is rapidly becoming an environment that takes full advantage of its graphical capabilities. If you roll your cursor over a linked word or picture, it may light up, wiggle, or become a three-dimensional image and rotate. Here's your first piece of surfing advice: Expect the unexpected, and keep a firm grip on your mouse. You never know what you'll find or what will link you to something else.

1 We're going to use the new default home page you set up in the last section to take a look at some of the different kinds of links that are out there. Click the Home button on the main button bar to bring up the PC/Computing page, if you don't see it already.

9 Now you're back where you started, and you used all kinds of links—buttons, menus, bars, and text—to make the journey.

8 Click the PC Computing link.

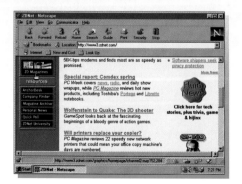

7 Find ZD Magazines on the Channels menu down the left side of the screen, and click on it.

● Always remember that the Web is a dynamic place. Web pages change all the time, sometimes from hour to hour, so even the images in this chapter may not match what you see on your screen.

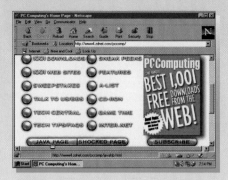

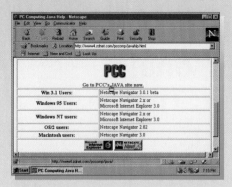

2 There are text, buttons, images, and bars on this page. Which ones are links? Roll your mouse around and find out: Both the words and the round, shiny buttons are links; you can tell because the arrow shape of your cursor becomes a pointing hand. Roll the mouse over to the Java Page link, and when you see the pointing hand, click your mouse button twice.

3 You should be able to see the moving red and blue PCC logo near the middle of the page—which means that Java is *enabled,* or turned on—so click on the underlined text that reads "Go to PCC's JAVA site now."

4 You've now arrived at PC/Computing's "Javacized" Web page, so move the cursor around to see what's different: When the cursor touches a button, for example, now it turns blue, and a description of where the button takes you pops up in the "torn" section of the page.

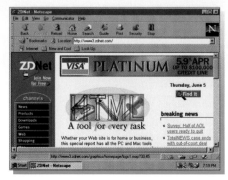

6 Now use ZD Net's button bar by clicking on ZDNet.

5 Use the scroll bar at the right of Netscape's window to scroll down and find the button bar at the bottom of the page. Click the ZD Net button, which takes you to ZD Net's home page.

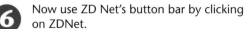

How to Surf Using the Personal Toolbar: The Internet

One of Communicator's new features is the Personal toolbar: the narrow toolbar at the bottom of the toolbar stack with three small icons on it. It is an excellent jumping-off point for your first official foray into the World Wide Web. We're going to start our investigation using the Internet icon, which links to Netscape's page of news, business, shopping, sports, and more. If you want to get a bird's eye view of what's going on in the world, this is the place to start.

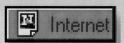

1 Click the first icon on the Personal toolbar: the tiny Netscape button labeled Internet. It takes you to Netscape's Guide, listing sites, news, and events on the Internet.

8 Finally, plan your next vacation with Travel by looking at maps and city guides, booking flights and hotels, even renting cars. For business or pleasure, it's here.

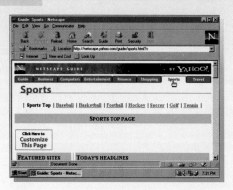

7 Sports provides scores, events, commentaries, professional and amateur sports information, and sports history.

● Take a look at the Customization feature on the main Guide page. Communicator enables you to tailor all the information covered on these pages to your personal tastes.

6 The Shopping tab provides access to sites of favorite vendors like Warner Brothers Studio Store, Lands End, JC Penney, and more. You can even apply for another credit card if you run out of cybercash during your spending spree.

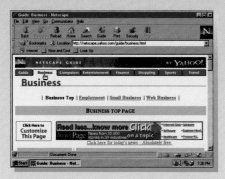

2 The Internet page is subdivided into several categories, as shown by the green thumbtabs along the top of the screen. Click the Business tab for reports on companies, marketing and advertising, personal finance, stocks and bonds, and more.

3 Click the Computers tab to feel the pulse of the Internet industry, with updates on media, products, software, and much more.

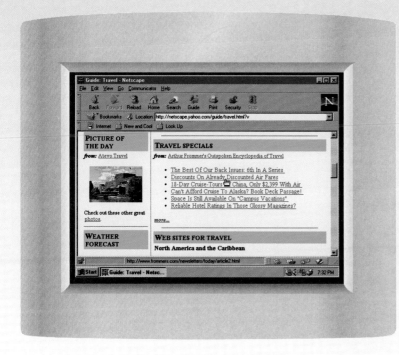

4 Click the Entertainment tab for the latest information on Hollywood, books, games, movies, music, television, and much more. You can visit Disney.com, Paramount Digital Entertainment, and other hot spots on the Web.

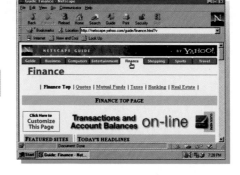

5 Click the Finance tab to consider banking, taxes, real estate, mutual funds, and whatever else your money is involved in.

How to Surf Using the Personal Toolbar: New and Cool

Now let's explore Netscape's hand-picked selection of Web sites that are new, cool, or both.

1 Click the second button on the Personal Toolbar: the New and Cool folder. From the submenu that appears, choose What's New.

● Remember your basic toolbar techniques: Back and Forward take you through the list of Web pages you've already visited, while Home brings you back to your home page.

● If you're a news hound, you may want to take advantage of Netscape's customized multimedia news service, In-Box Direct. This free Netscape feature will deliver rich, interactive Web pages directly to your e-mail in-box, including pictures, video, sound, and active links. To register, look for the phrase "In-Box Direct" or for the mailbox with the *N* on the lid on Netscape's home page.

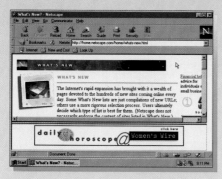

3 Click the Guide button again, and this time choose What's Cool.

2 The What's New page is the place to visit if you are interested in browsing a list of completely new Web sites. As you can see, the subject matter is unlimited, so you never know what you may find here.

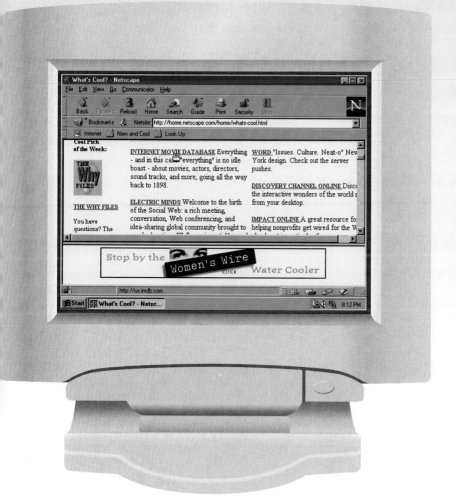

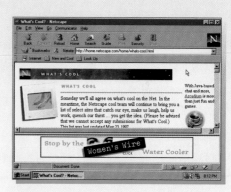

4 This list of sites is a collection of pages or locations on the Web that are "cool": Perhaps the subject matter is interesting or new to the Web, or the site makes use of cutting-edge technology, or the design is fresh and innovative. Take some time to browse around these sites and see some of the best the Web has to offer.

How to Surf Using the Personal Toolbar: Look Up

The third and last button on the Personal toolbar is the Look Up button. You can use it to quickly access white and yellow pages sites, where you can search for a person, phone number, e-mail address, street address, or business—anywhere in the world.

1 Click the third button on the Personal Toolbar: the Look Up folder. From the sub-menu that appears, choose People.

● There are many yellow and white pages available on the World Wide Web, and you'll get a glimpse of some of them in this section. Remember, you'll have the opportunity to get a closer look in the next part of the book.

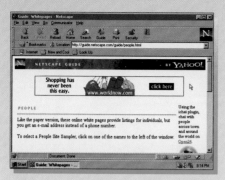

2 The People white pages site enables you to search many popular white pages on the Internet in order to find someone's e-mail address, phone number, and so on. Searching with white pages will be covered in more detail later on in this section of the book—for now, just have a brief look around.

3 Now return to the Personal toolbar and click the Look Up folder icon again. This time when the submenu appears, choose Yellow Pages.

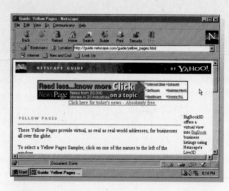

4 Netscape's Yellow Pages page lets you access many different national and international yellow pages. You can search for a business or corporation by location, street address, or name. You can also use 3-D yellow pages to see your listing in virtual reality, and you can search business-related classified ads. It's all here in one place. (There's also going to be a more extensive look at how to use yellow pages later on in this section of the book, so again, just briefly look around for now.)

How to Interpret Error Messages

As you find your way across the Web, you'll inevitably run into many error messages. Error messages result from a variety of situations, some relating to Netscape, others due to how the Internet operates. Sometimes you'll see an error message because the Web site you want can't handle a large number of simultaneous visits. Or sometimes a Web page has moved or no longer exists. Netscape will most often try to evaluate the situation and present you with a solution, but it isn't always so easy. You may have to try again later, or try another Web site altogether to find the information you're seeking.

1 A "Data Missing" message most often occurs when you're using the Back button to get back to a Web page you've already visited. If you get this message, Navigator has dropped the Web page you want from its cache. If you click the Reload button on the main toolbar, Navigator will download it again.

8 A "Bad Request" message is exactly that: Something in the way you've requested access to a Web site isn't quite right, and the server can't understand what you want.

7 A "Fatal Error" message does not mean that your computer is about to self-destruct or that you've somehow damaged the Internet. It's simply another, even stronger warning that you don't have permission to access that particular Web site.

● You can always find your way around an error message or being denied access to a Web site by using the Back button on the main toolbar to retrace your steps. If you're looking for sites on a particular subject, try another site. If you're simply surfing to see the sights, move on to something else.

2 If you've gotten a "Data Missing" message by using a search engine, like one of the search engines you discovered through Netscape's Destinations page, Netscape will ask if you want to "Repost form data?" This data is the result of your search engine request, so go ahead and click OK.

3 The "No DNS" error message can mean a couple of things: You may have typed in the site address, or *URL*, incorrectly, or perhaps the site no longer exists. It is also possible, though, that too many people are trying to visit this site at the same time. In this situation, it always pays to come back and try again—but if you get this error message two or three times, chances are the site is gone.

4 Sometimes you'll get a request for a user name and password, which means you've accessed a private site and won't be able to get in without this information. Use the Back button to retrace your steps and try another Web site.

Fatal Error 403

Access forbidden:

6 The "Error 404" message means a Web site definitely doesn't exist because it's been moved or deleted. Are you getting the hang of that Back button yet?

5 The "Error 401" message is a lot like the previous message, except that you're given no chance whatsoever to access this site. Again, click the Back button on the main toolbar and take another route.

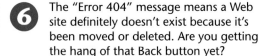

How to Use an Index: Yahoo!

The first kind of search tool created for the Web was the *index*, which is a listing of Web sites by a set of categories. Yahoo! became extremely popular (and its founders very wealthy) because it was the best of the bunch, presenting Web surfers with a list of logical, well-organized categories most people could understand. If you have a good idea of what you're looking for and what it's called or where it's located, an index could be the best place for you to begin your search.

1 To go to Yahoo!'s home page, click the *N* or Netscape button, choose Netscape Destinations from the green button bar, and scroll down to the second Destinations text menu. Click Net Search and then click Yahoo!.

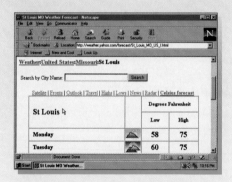

7 Scroll down the Yahoo! St. Louis Forecast page and click IntelliCast: St. Louis Weather. It's not necessarily a nice outlook, but the information is nicely presented.

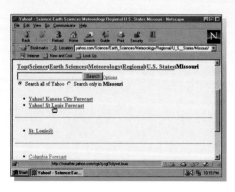

6 Almost there: Click Yahoo! St. Louis Forecast.

FYI

● If the URL you want to enter is like Yahoo!'s—a single word (*yahoo*) preceded by *www.* and followed by *.com*—Navigator can save you some typing. Click once in the Location bar at the top of Navigator's screen, and, to use Yahoo! as an example, simply type yahoo and press Enter. Navigator will do the rest, and take you to the place you want to go.

2 Let's say you want to find tomorrow's forecast and you live in St. Louis. Select Weather from the main Yahoo! menu.

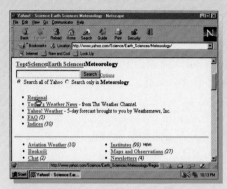

3 You can see that Yahoo! is automatically narrowing your search as you go. Click on Regional.

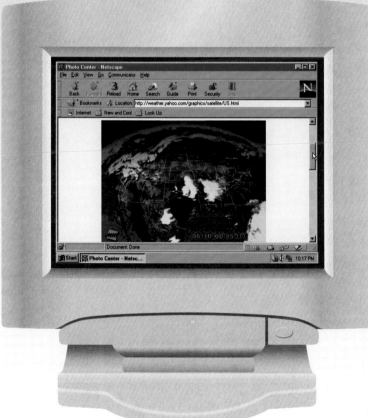

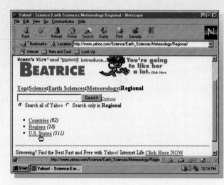

4 Now narrow the search even further by clicking on U.S. States.

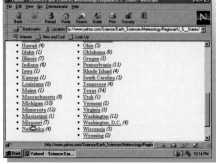

5 What state do you want? Click Missouri, which, as you can see from the number next to it, has seven related Web sites to choose from.

How to Use a Search Engine: Lycos

If you're looking for information on a certain subject, but you don't know where to begin, using a search engine is your best bet. A *search engine* is different from an index (such as Yahoo!) because it lets you access the entire World Wide Web, rather than providing a short list of specific sites that may or may not contain what you want. With a search engine like Lycos, you can enter a few keywords and one or two criteria, and come up with hundreds of possible starting points.

1 Open a Location box using the File menu or the shortcut keys and type in **Lycos**. Navigator will automatically extend the URL to **www.lycos.com** and take you to Lycos's home page.

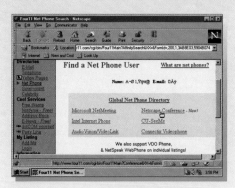

7 The last search button on Lycos's button bar is Search Help, the place to go for help on how to use Lycos. Find out more about how to customize the search you just completed, or begin another.

● **Be as specific as you can with your keywords. If you're looking for a music store in Denver, but you only type** music, **you're going to get a listing of thousands of music sites all over the world. Type** music stores Denver, **instead, to keep your search narrow.**

● **Although every search engine works on the same principle—retrieving information based on the keywords you enter—they all "think" a little differently. So if you don't get the results you want with one search engine, keep trying others until you find the one you like best.**

6 Clicking the next button, Search Sounds, brings back 63 pages, all with potential sound clips from radio interviews, records, and concerts.

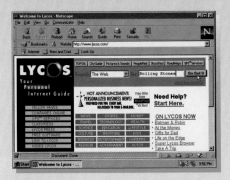

2 Say you're looking for Web pages about the British supergroup The Rolling Stones. Click in the for: location box and type **Rolling Stones**, then click the Go Get It button to begin your search.

3 Lycos comes back with over 11,000 possibilities, sorted by *confidence,* or percentage points. Lycos has guessed that the first item on the list, the Rolling Stones Guest Comment Log, has a 100% chance of being exactly what you want because the first two words in the title match...but it's not what you're looking for.

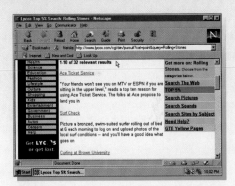

4 Scroll up to the button bar near the top of the page and click Related Sites. This brings up a different sorting of Web sites about The Rolling Stones, and the first one—Stonesworld—is definitely more similar to what you want.

5 Now click the Pictures button on Lycos's button bar. Lycos comes back with 51 sites containing pictures of the band—concert photos, magazine poses, promotional shots, and more.

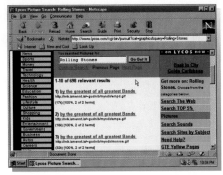

How to Use White Pages: Four11

Have you lost contact with a friend from school, or forgotten someone's e-mail address? A white pages site like Four11 can help you out. White pages work like other keyword-searchable listings, but you use a person's first and last names; their location by city, state, and country; and other Web-specific information to considerably narrow your search before it even begins. In this section, you'll look for a particular person with a common last name to illustrate the features and functionality of a white pages listing.

1 Open Four11's home page by clicking in the Location box, typing **four11**, and pressing Enter.
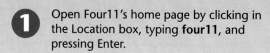

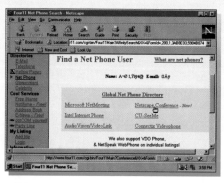

● Notice that Four11 has a little check box in the e-mail search window called SmartName. This is in case your friend Bob's information is listed under Bobby Smith or Robert Smith. If you check SmartName, Four11 will pull numbers up that are listed under all three names.

6 You can also use Four11's Directories listings to find an organization's NetPhone number, to find government information, and to find a way to contact your favorite celebrity.

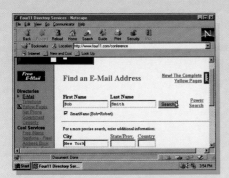

2 You're going to look for your friend Bob Smith, who lives in New York City. Type in the right information in the right spots and click the Search button.

3 There he is! Your first search was a success.

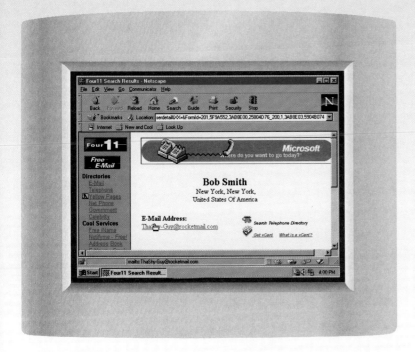

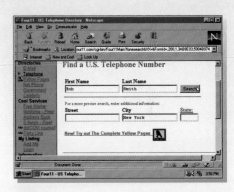

4 Now use the Directories menu on the left side of the page and click Telephone. You can't remember Bob's phone number, either, so type in the same information and click Search again.

5 Success again!

How to Use Yellow Pages: BigBook

What's the difference between a white pages listing and a yellow pages listing? It's just like a phone book: Internet white pages list individuals and Internet yellow pages list businesses. If you're using a Web version of a yellow pages listing, you can search for businesses and companies all over the world, not just in your neighborhood. In this section, you'll use a popular yellow pages listing called BigBook to look for antique shops in Tampa, Florida. Why? Because you can—there are no boundaries on the Internet.

1 To go to BigBook's Web site, click in the Location box, type **bigbook**, and press Enter. Navigator will do the rest.

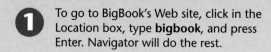

5 BigBook has other handy features accessible through its main button bar at the top of the screen. Click Your Book, for example, to build your own customized yellow pages, or click Business Center if you want to use BigBook to market your own business.

● If you need more help with your search on BigBook, choose the Categories button near the Search button for a complete listing of BigBook's categories. There are also ways to extend or customize your search process by using the Advanced Search page, which you can link to via the More Search Options button.

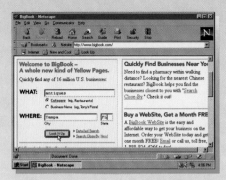

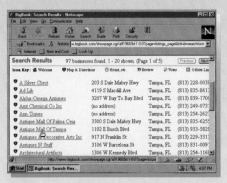

2 You're looking for antique shops in the Tampa, Florida, area, so click in the What: window and type **antiques**, then click in the Where: window and type **Tampa**. Enter **FL**, the abbreviation for Florida, in the State window. Click Search Now to begin.

3 BigBook comes back with 97 possibilities. You don't want to drive all over creation, so click the Antique Mall of Tampa link. BigBook gives you the address, location, and phone number of the mall, along with a general list of what is sold there.

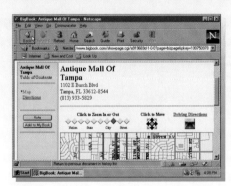

4 Click the Back button on the main toolbar to go back to the previous page. You're also interested in Aspree Antiques, but you don't know where it is. Click the tiny green square to the left; BigBook will give you directions to help you get to Aspree, from your house or the mall if you so desire.

How to Find Shareware and Freeware: Shareware.com

*S*hareware and *freeware* are software programs you can download from the Internet for free or for a reasonable registration fee. At CNET's Shareware.com site, you can do keyword searches for shareware or freeware for your specific kind of computer, you can read reviews or recommendations on the top software, and you can browse a new arrivals list.

1 To get to Shareware.com, click in the Location box, type **shareware.com**, and press Enter.

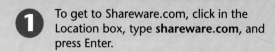

8 Now a Saving Location dialog box will appear, where you can watch your shareware or freeware being downloaded from the Internet.

7 Windows will present you with the Save As dialog box. Click the Save button to begin downloading the tax program.

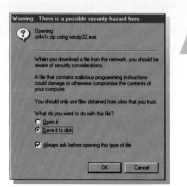

6 An Unknown File Type dialog box will appear. Click the Save it to disk button.

● Remember to check out the back inside cover of the book for a comprehensive list of keyboard shortcuts.

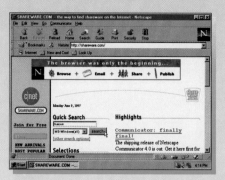

2 Let's do a Quick Search for something to help with calculating taxes. Click in the Quick Search box and type **taxes**. Now go to the pull-down menu just below to choose your platform. Make sure MS-Windows (all) is selected (at the top of the list), then click the Search button.

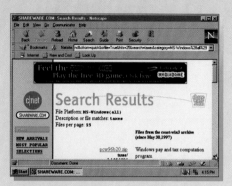

3 Your search comes back with 25 choices: There are programs here for individual or joint personal taxes, a pay and tax computator, and more.

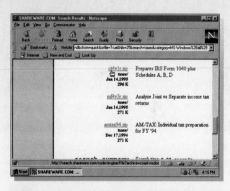

4 Scroll down til you find the link named ot4v1r.zip. The description reads, "Prepares IRS form 1040 plus Schedules A, B, D." Very handy.

5 Click the ot4v1r.zip link, and a list appears of download sites around the world. You always want to choose the site that's closest to you geographically. On this list, scroll down to the bottom of the page under USA. Click the first link, FTP.agt.net.

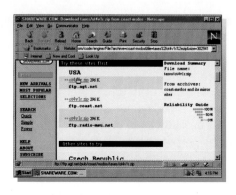

How to Add and Save a Bookmark

In your Web travels, you'll come across lots of garbage. You'll see sites that are so poorly designed that you'll wonder why people went to the trouble to put them online in the first place. But for every awful site you find, you'll discover others that you enjoy and admire. And saving the URLs of these great sites is a piece of cake with Navigator's Bookmarks.

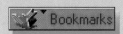

1 After launching Navigator, look for the Bookmarks folder button on Navigator's Location toolbar (the middle toolbar, just below the main toolbar). Click this button and the Bookmarks pull-down menu will appear.

7 For practice, now click the *N* or Netscape button and add Netscape's home page to your Bookmarks file by following the steps in this exercise again. Then you'll have three bookmarks to work with in the next lesson.

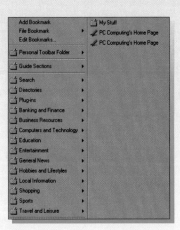

6 Now click the Bookmarks icon again, and you'll see the PC Computing Web site bookmarked twice. (We'll remove the second, unnecessary bookmark later in this section.)

FYI

● The Guide button on the main toolbar is a short Bookmarks file all its own, with permanent, built-in links to a short list of Netscape's most interesting Web pages. You cannot add or delete these "bookmarks," but they do provide a fast and easy link to these three popular areas of Netscape's Web site.

2 At the top of the menu there are three choices: Add Bookmark, File Bookmark, and Edit Bookmarks. Select Add Bookmark—we're going to add the PC/Computing Web site as a bookmark.

3 Now click the Bookmarks icon again, and you'll see PC/Computing's home page saved as your first bookmark at the very bottom of the menu. Scroll down the Bookmarks pull-down menu and select the PC/Computing bookmark.

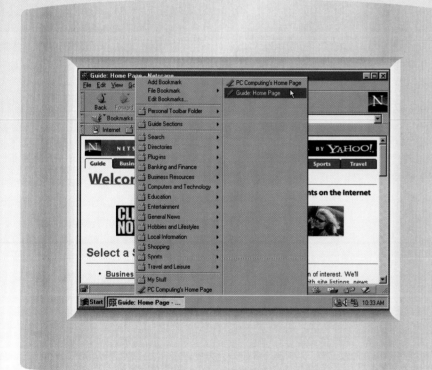

4 The PC/Computing home page loads up again, which tells you the bookmark works.

5 The second easy way to create a bookmark is to click the tiny green and yellow icon to the left of the Location window. If you roll the cursor over it, it wiggles and a balloon appears saying, "Drag this to create a link to this page." Click and drag this icon to the Bookmark icon to save the URL displayed in the Location window—PC Computing's home page—as a bookmark.

How to Edit Your Bookmark File

In this lesson, you'll learn the basic capabilities of Navigator's Bookmarks file. You'll explore the pull-down menus within the Bookmarks management window, learn a few simple tasks, and become familiar with the general window layout.

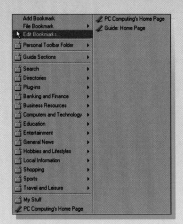

 1 After you've launched Navigator, click the Bookmarks button and choose Edit Bookmarks from the Bookmarks menu.

 6 Now if you return to the Bookmark menu and select Computers and Publications, you'll see the PC Computing home page has been saved again in a more appropriate folder. (Go ahead and delete the other PC Computing bookmark at the bottom of the menu so you have it listed only once.)

● **You can open and close folders within your Bookmarks file by clicking the tiny plus and minus boxes to the left of each folder icon: A minus sign means the folder is open and you can see the bookmarks stored inside, and a plus sign means the folder is closed.**

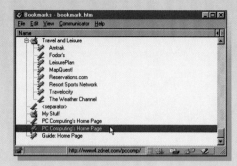

2 Let's remove the second PC Computing bookmark. In the new window that appears, which shows all the individual bookmarks in your Bookmark file, scroll down to the very bottom to the two PC Computing bookmarks. Click the second bookmark, and press the Delete key on your keyboard. Close the window when you're done.

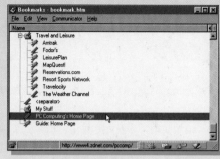

3 Now you're left with two bookmarks in your Bookmark list—the first and only PC Computing entry and the Netscape home page entry.

4 You can organize your bookmarks with the Bookmark folder categories. Open the Bookmark menu and click File Bookmark.

5 This is actually a third way to bookmark a Web site. You should be at PC Computing magazine's Web site (go there if you're not); now select Computers and Technology on the File Bookmark submenu.

How to Import and Export Bookmark Lists

This lesson covers a brand new feature of Netscape Communicator 4.0: importing and exporting bookmark lists. *Importing* a bookmark list means picking it up from a place on your computer like your desktop, your e-mail inbox, a disk, or elsewhere. *Exporting* a bookmark list means just the reverse: saving it to a disk, placing it on your desktop, e-mailing it to another person, and so forth. The idea is to make a bookmark list portable and independent from Navigator, just like any other document you create on your computer.

1 After launching Navigator, open the Bookmarks menu and choose Edit Bookmarks.

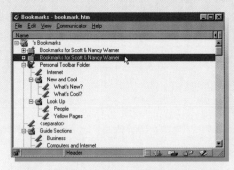

7 Before you move on, remove the duplicate folder by highlighting it (here it's the second Bookmarks for Scott & Nancy Warner) and pressing the Delete key.

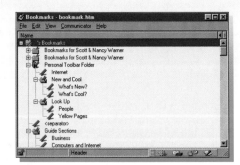

6 Now it looks like you're seeing double, but you get the idea: You've just successfully added a group of links to your Bookmarks file without having to visit each individual site.

● Notice that the name of each bookmark on your Bookmarks list is the same as the words that appear at the very top of Navigator's window, and not necessarily the name of the Web site itself. This title is decided when the Web page is designed; it's a customizable feature, but it's not something you can change on your end at this point.

2 Let's export the Bookmarks list you already created. In the Bookmarks dialog box, open the File menu and choose Save As.

3 The Save Bookmarks File dialog box appears. Choose where you want to save the file (for instance, the Navigator folder on your hard drive), then in the File Name window, type **bookmark2**, and click the Save button. You've just exported a copy of your original bookmark file to your hard drive.

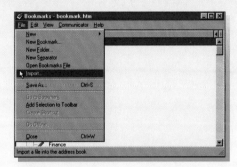

4 Now to reverse the process and import the bookmarks file, open the File menu again, but this time choose Import.

5 The Import Bookmarks File dialog box appears. Click on the file named bookmark2, then click the Open button.

P A R T 3

Using Messenger: Managing E-Mail

MESSENGER is a powerful e-mail management program that allows you to do much more than receive and reply to e-mail messages. It lets you save and sort e-mail in several different ways according to your personal preferences, and helps you sift through unwanted e-mail to get to what's important to you.

Messenger can import and deliver e-mail including all kinds of attachments—text, pictures, audio and video, bookmark lists and more—and/or active hypertext links. It can also incorporate security features like encryption if you're worried about sending vital information that needs to be encrypted.

IN THIS SECTION YOU'LL LEARN

How to Use Messenger's Main Toolbar

Messenger is a completely different program than Navigator, with its own toolbars, pull-down menus, and other tools and capabilities. In this section you'll be introduced to the tools on Messenger's Toolbar, just as you were introduced to Navigator.

1 The Get Message button downloads new e-mail messages from the server.

9 Finally, the Stop button stops a download in progress if you change your mind.

8 The Delete button is your trash can—highlight the message you want to throw away by clicking it once and pressing this button.

2 The New Message button brings up a blank form so you can write a new e-mail message.

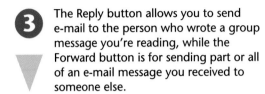

3 The Reply button allows you to send e-mail to the person who wrote a group message you're reading, while the Forward button is for sending part or all of an e-mail message you received to someone else.

4 The File button saves the message you're reading to a folder in your Inbox so you can sort the e-mail you keep.

5 The Next button let you scroll through your un-read messages.

7 The Security button keeps you updated on your security status.

6 The Print button lets you print an e-mail message on paper just like a regular word processing document.

How to Use Messenger's Other Buttons

As in the new version of Navigator, Messenger has a second set of buttons scattered all over its open Window. These new buttons greatly extend your control and management capabilities, and allow you to integrate Messenger's functions with other programs in Communicator.

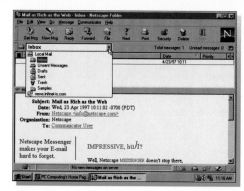

1 When you click the Folder pull-down menu button, Messenger opens a pull-down menu listing all your e-mail and newsgroup folders and the trash folder. This is a quick, alternative way to look at your new and saved e-mail messages.

9 Finally, the Security padlock icon in the lower left corner will provide you with security information if you click it once. Security issues will be covered more completely in Part 7.

8 The open/close tab to the left of the Taskbar moves this toolbar alternatively off and back onto the Messenger window. Clicking the tab in either spot moves this toolbar to the other position.

● Remember that you can always look at the status bar toward the left bottom corner of Messenger's window if you want a short description of a tool or button. Roll the cursor over the button you'd like described, and the corresponding message will appear in the status bar.

2 Clicking the Message Center Button opens the Message Center window—this is where you can easily create new e-mail folders for sorting saved e-mail, compose new e-mail messages, and more.

3 The Mailbox toolbar details many kinds of information about the messages in your Inbox—Subject, Sender, Date Received, Priority, Status, Message Length, and more. Clicking each individual button resorts your messages accordingly, and the arrow buttons on the right end of the toolbar allow you to see as many or as few of these categories as you like.

4 The Composer button—the last of four on the Component bar—opens Composer. Remember you'll explore Composer in depth in Part 6.

5 The Discussion Groups button also links you to the Message Center. You'll learn more about Collabra in Part 4.

6 The Mailbox button is how you got to Messenger in the first place.

7 The Navigator button automatically opens a new browser window in Navigator.

How to Use Messenger's File Pull-Down Menu

L ike the File pull-down menu in Navigator, the Messenger File menu provides you with some common and easy-to-use functions that you can access with the click of a mouse. Use the File pull-down menu to open a Navigator browser window, open a page in Composer or a new URL location on the Web, to close and save e-mail messages, and more.

1 To open the File pull-down menu, click File once and move the cursor down to choose from the available options.

7 Close closes the Message Center, and Exit is the way to leave Messenger and Navigator and close all open windows.

6 Go Offline lets you disconnect from the Internet while reading and sorting your e-mail and newsgroup postings. (You do have to be online to send e-mail and postings, though.)

● **The Message Center is the heart of both Messenger and of Collabra, as it is the place where you store, sort, and otherwise manage all your e-mail and newsgroup postings. So don't be surprised when you return to this part of Communicator in Part 4 when you learn how to use Collabra.**

2 The New pull-down menu contains the Navigator Window, which opens a blank window in Navigator; Message, which opens a blank e-mail form; and Blank Page; Page From Template; and Page From Wizard; three Web page authoring choices.

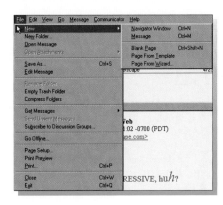

3 New Discussion Group, New Discussion Group Server, and Open Discussion Group are all Collabra features which will be thoroughly discussed in Part 4.

4 New Folder, Empty Trash Folder, and Compress Folders are all e-mail management tasks you'll learn about in the Part 4.

5 Get Messages and Send Unsent Messages are sending and receiving functions you'll use later on in this part of the book. Subscribe to Discussion Groups is another Collabra feature discussed in Part 4.

How to Use Messenger's Edit Pull-Down Menu

Messenger's Edit pull-down menu is a collection of e-mail composition choices. Once you've typed out a new e-mail message, or if you're reading an existing message, the Edit tools let you cut, copy, and paste sections; delete and select individual messages for replying; search messages in your inbox and your phone book; and change the setup and mail filter rules.

1 To open the Edit pull-down menu, click Edit once and roll the cursor down to choose from the available options.

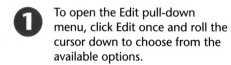

7 You'll remember seeing Preferences before, from Navigator's Edit menu. You can access your Mail & Groups preferences settings here without having to return to Navigator.

FYI

● As with previous pull-down menus in both Navigator and in Messenger, you'll find some menu options will be highlighted or usable, and others will be unhighlighted or not usable. This constantly changes as you read, sort, delete, decode, and browse through your different kinds of e-mail. Just remember that Messenger will provide you with all the menu options you'll need as you go.

3 Delete Message lets you throw a message in the trash and Select Message chooses various groups of messages.

2 Undo, Redo, Cut, Copy, and Paste all permit you to manipulate highlighted sections of text in an e-mail message. None of these choices are highlighted in the Edit menu at the moment because you have no message open. Delete Message lets you throw a highlighted message away right from the Inbox, so it is highlighted here on the menu.

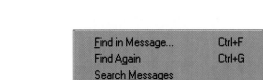

4 The next four menu capabilities—Find in Message, Find Again, Search Messages, and Search Directory—let you search your Inbox as you'd search an index: by keyword or phrase.

Manage Mail Account
Manage Discussion Group

5 Manage Mail Account and Manage Discussion Group allow you change your password, set up mail forwarding, and/or send vacation notices. You might find these features useful if you won't be reading e-mail or newsgroup postings for a while and you don't want your Inbox to be flooded.

 6 Mail Filters is an automatic sorting feature you'll explore later on in the book, and Properties gives you more information about a selected message or posting.

How to Use Messenger's View Pull-Down Menu

Messenger's View pull-down menu allows you to control how you look at Inbox display and at e-mail messages. You can use this menu to hide or display the main toolbar; to automatically hide or display highlighted e-mail messages; to sort e-mail messages by thread, header, or attachment; and more.

1 To open the View pull-down menu, click View once and roll the cursor down to choose from the available options.

8 Encoding, as in Navigator, is something you'd use if your e-mail is/was written in a non-Western alphabet (like Russian or Chinese).

● As with previous pull-down menus in both Navigator and in Messenger, you'll find some menu options will be highlighted or usable, and others will be unhighlighted or not usable. This constantly changes as you read, sort, delete, decode, and browse through your different kinds of e-mail. Just remember that Messenger will provide you with all the menu options you'll need as you go.

Page Source
Page Info

7 Page Source and Page Info are, again, features you may find useful after learning how to use Composer and/or after exploring Netscape's security features in Parts 6 and 7 respectively.

Hide _N_avigation Toolbar
Hide _L_ocation Toolbar
Show _C_ategories
Hide Messa_g_e

2 Hide/Show Navigation Toolbar and Hide/Show Location Toolbar allow you to hide or reveal these toolbars if you choose. Show/Hide Categories and Show/Hide Message work on the same principle, only with mail categories and individual mail messages.

So_r_t   ▶
_M_essages   ▶
Hea_d_ers   ▶
_A_ttachments   ▶

3 Sort, Messages, Headers, and Attachments are all different e-mail categorization and management tools you'll learn more about later on in this part of the book.

Increase _F_ont   Ctrl+]
Decrease Fon_t_   Ctrl+[

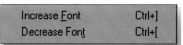

4 Increase Font and Decrease Font allow you to enlarge or reduce the size of e-mail text for easier reading or to fit more text in the open window.

_R_eload
Sho_w_ Images
Re_f_resh
_S_top Loading   ESC

5 Reload, Show Images, and Refresh work just the same way as they did in Navigator, only here in Messenger, you use them with e-mail messages instead of Web pages. Stop Loading will stop a message or graphic from being retrieved after you have requested it.

U_n_scramble (ROT13)
Wra_p_ Long Lines

6 Unscramble is a security feature used to read encrypted, or coded, e-mail, and Wrap Long Lines arranges text to make it fit within the open Messenger window.

How to Use Messenger's Go Pull-Down Menu

Messenger's Go pull-down menu allows you to move back, forth, and among different items in your Inbox. You can use this menu to browse messages, threads, and—when you get to Part 4 where we'll cover Netscape Collabra—newsgroup posts.

1 To open the Go pull-down menu, click Go once and move the cursor down to choose from the available options.

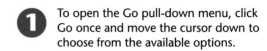

6 Finally, Back and Forward involve sorting both unread and previously read messages, which you'll explore in the next chapter. Remember that these unhighlighted menu options will darken or become highlighted when and if you need them.

● As with previous pull-down menus in both Navigator and in Messenger, you'll find some menu options will be highlighted or usable, and others will be unhighlighted or not usable. This constantly changes as you read, sort, delete, de-code, and browse through your different kinds of e-mail. Just remember that Messenger will provide you with all the menu options you'll need as you go.

2 Next Message, Next Unread Message, and Next Flagged Message allow you to move up and down a list of e-mail messages in your Inbox. (You may find it easier to simply point-and-click the specific message in your Inbox you wish to read.)

3 Next Category and Next Unread Category let you browse e-mail messages within a single category—something you'll learn more about later on in this part of the book.

4 Next Newsgroup and Next Unread Newsgroup are Collabra functions you'll explore in Part 4.

5 Previous Message, Previous Unread Message, and Previous Flagged Message are similar to the first three pull-down menu items, except that they allow you to move up the list instead of down. First Flagged Message moves you to the top of a flagged list of messages.

How to Use Messenger's Message Pull-Down Menu

If you want a concise list of all the ways you can use and manage your e-mail, open the Message pull-down menu. You can retrieve, send, respond, reply, forward, quote, file, copy, mark and flag—and more—all from this one place in Messenger.

 To open the Message pull-down menu, click Message once and roll the cursor down to choose from the available options.

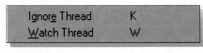

 Ignore Thread and Watch Thread let you read or disregard all e-mail in your box that deals with one subject.

● As with previous pull-down menus in both Navigator and in Messenger, you'll find some menu options will be highlighted or usable, and others will be unhighlighted or not usable. This constantly changes as you read, sort, delete, decode, and browse through your different kinds of e-mail. Just remember that Messenger will provide you with all the menu options you'll need as you go.

Mark lets you read or save e-mail in a number of ways, while Flag and Unflag will be covered later on.

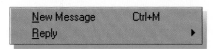

2 New Message brings up the new message window for writing e-mail, and Reply lets you respond in four different, shortcutted ways.

3 Forward and Forward Quoted allow you to send an e-mail message you've received to another person.

4 Add to Address Book lets you add an individual or a group of people to your Address Book in a few mouse clicks.

5 File Message and Copy Message both let you move e-mail to one of the same five folders—Inbox, Outbox, Drafts, Sent, or Trash.

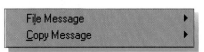

How to Use Messenger's Communicator Pull-Down Menu

The Communicator menu in Netscape Messenger is virtually the same as the Communicator menu in Navigator—it helps you easily move among the five parts of Communicator (Navigator, Messenger, Composer, Collabra, and Conference).

1 To open the Communicator pull-down menu, click Communicator once and move the cursor down to choose from the available options.

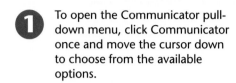

9 Java Console is an advanced Web page building feature you may use if you become an advanced Web page designer.

8 Finally, at the bottom of the Window menu there is a list of all the Web pages you've visited during your current session, listed in chronological order. Here, you've only been one place so you have only one location.

FYI

● As with previous pull-down menus in both Navigator and Messenger, you'll find some menu options will be highlighted or usable, and others will be unhighlighted or not usable. This constantly changes as you read, sort, delete, decode, and browse through your different kinds of e-mail. Just remember that Messenger will provide you with all the menu options you'll need as you go.

2 Navigator opens a new Navigator window; Messenger Mailbox opens your e-mail; Collabra Discussions Groups opens your newsgroup postings; Page Composer opens a blank Web page; and Conference launches Communicator's long distance calling program (there's more on these other components in Parts 3, 4, 5, 6, and 7, respectively).

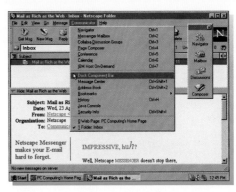

3 Show/Dock Component Bar determines the location of the button bar in the lower right corner of Navigator's window—in the center figure in this section, it's "docked," but here it's "shown."

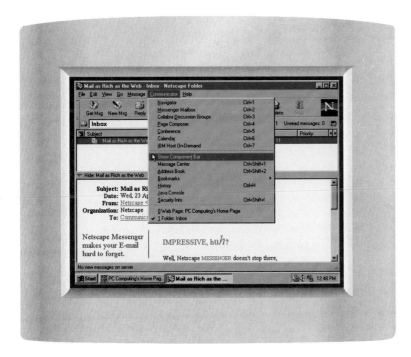

4 Message Center opens your e-mail and newsgroups message center, which will be explained more thoroughly later in Part 3 and in Part 4.

5 Address Book will be a list of e-mail addresses and newsgroups you write to frequently—you'll establish it later in this Part.

7 History is a detailed, more technical list of all the sites you've visited during your current session. For now, you may feel satisfied with the list at the end of this menu, which is close to the same thing.

6 Bookmarks is a way to memorize and keep the URLs or addresses of Web pages you want to visit many times.

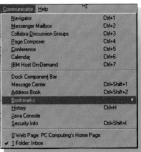

How to Use Messenger's Help Menu

The Help menu is one of Navigator's best features for the new user. You may remember using some of these features earlier to register your Netscape Communicator software with Netscape and to get technical support. This section explores all the Help menu items in greater detail.

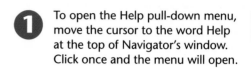

1 To open the Help pull-down menu, move the cursor to the word Help at the top of Navigator's window. Click once and the menu will open.

8 About Communicator, the last item on the Help menu, is some legal jargon that you may or may not want to read. Either way, you've finished looking at the Help menu and the entire set of pull-down menus. Now you're on your way.

FYI

● Never type an e-mail message using all capital letters (LIKE THIS). In cyberspace, it means you're shouting—and it makes what you've written much harder to read.

● For courtesy, always put something in the Subject line of your message that describes what you're writing about, even if the recipient is someone you know well or is expecting your message.

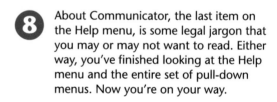

7 About Font Displayers touches on questions concerning dynamic text and other, similar subjects.

2 If you want to read about Navigator's various features and capabilities, you would click Help Contents, Release Notes, and/or Product Information and Support. We will explore how to use Help Contents, or NetHelp, in one of the Projects at the end of the book.

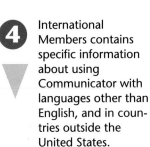

3 We've already checked out Software Updates and Register Now in Part 1, and Member Services contains the same type of information.

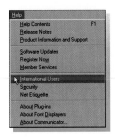

4 International Members contains specific information about using Communicator with languages other than English, and in countries outside the United States.

5 Security is covered in depth in Part 7 along with other security issues, and Net Etiquette provides newcomers to the Internet with an outline of basic online manners.

6 About Plug-ins is a list of audio, video, and other multimedia components already installed on your computer with Navigator.

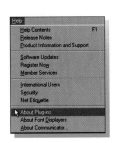

How to Create and Send a New E-Mail Message

In this lesson, you'll learn how to create and send an e-mail message using quick and easy functions in Netscape Messenger. E-mail, short for *electronic mail*, has quickly become an integral part of many people's lives, both inside and outside the office. No matter who you are, what you do, or where your interests lie, learning to send, receive, and manage e-mail will greatly enhance your experiences on the Internet.

1 The easiest way to create a new e-mail message is to click the New Msg button on the main toolbar, or press Ctrl+M. This opens up the Message Composition box.

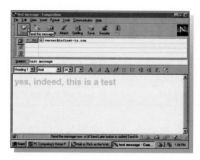

8 Now look at your message text: looks different, doesn't it? For the finale, click the Send button on the main toolbar. You've just completed your first task using Netscape Messenger with style.

7 Finally, open the Color pull-down menu (it's in the middle of the same toolbar, very inconspicuous) and choose Blue Green when the palette opens.

● Because e-mail is a widely used form of communication for both business and extra-curricular uses, there are certain rules of "netiquette" you'll want to follow. Always treat people courteously even if they are rude or insulting to you. And, especially if you're writing e-mail in a business environment, mind your manners: swear words, off-color remarks, and tasteless jokes aren't appreciated in meetings so they're not appropriate in your work-related messages.

2 For purposes of this exercise, you're going to write and send a message to yourself. The cursor is already flashing in the Address line, so type in your own e-mail address.

3 In the middle of the box there is a blank area named Subject. Click once in the box provided and type **test message**.

4 Now click once in the large blank white area in the bottom half of the window. This is where you put your message: for now type **yes, indeed, this is a test**. The Enter, Backspace, and other typing keys on your keyboard still work the same way if you type as badly as I do.

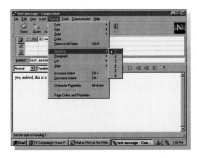

6 Now click and drag the entire message and open the Font pull-down menu. Choose Arial, and you've changed the kind of letters Messenger uses to display your message.

5 Let's play around with this boring little message to demonstrate Messenger's formatting options. Open the Format pull-down menu and choose Heading 1. Now your message text is huge.

How to Retrieve and Answer E-Mail

N ow that you've sent yourself an e-mail message, it's time learn how to retrieve it from your Internet service provider and how to write a reply.

1 You're going to work with the message you sent to yourself, so click the Get Mail button once. Messenger will see if you have new mail—and you do. It appears listed in the Inbox.

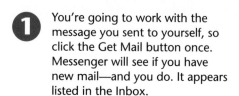

7 Close both the second and the first test message windows by choosing Close from the File pull-down menu, or pressing Ctrl+W.

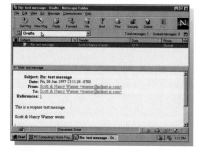

6 Ordinarily you would press the Send button as you did in the last exercise. This time, however, click the Save button on the main toolbar as we're going to use this message in the next lesson. If you open the Draft folder, you'll see this message has been saved there for you to send at a later time.

FYI

● Messenger will always automatically save a copy of any e-mail message you send to your Sent folder. You never have to manually save a message to another or mail yourself a copy, but it's a good idea to sort your Sent mail every so often.

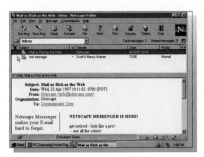

2 Click the e-mail's entry displayed in the Inbox—this is the easiest way to open a message.

3 Here's your message. Let's send a response.

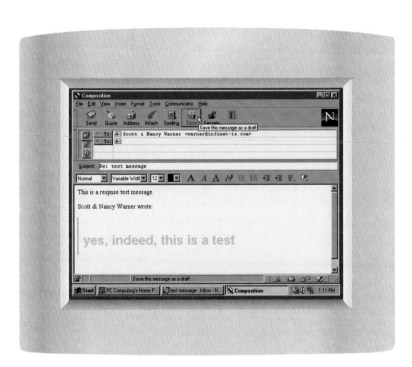

4 Click the Re:Mail button on the main toolbar to create a response. Choose Reply to Sender as it's not a group message.

5 A new Message Composition box opens. The sender's e-mail address is already provided, and the Subject line reads "Re: test message." In the body space, type **This is a response test message**.

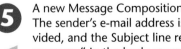

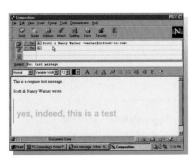

How to Quote and Forward E-Mail

Whe you're sending and responding to e-mail, you'll want to refer to something you've already read, or you'll want to pass on something you've received to another person. This is what *quoting* and *forwarding* are for.

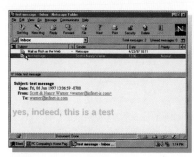

1 First, open the "test message" e-mail in your Inbox by double-clicking it. You must have the message you want to quote already open on your desktop.

7 Double-click "[Fwd:test message]" to open it. This is what a *forwarded* message looks like—your comments are listed first above the bar, and the forwarded information is listed below it. Delete this message, too, by clicking the Delete button again.

6 Double-click "test message 2" to open it. This is what a *quoted* message looks like—the quote, minus the fancy stuff, is offset by the brackets, while the response you wrote to it appears just below. Delete this message by clicking the Delete button on the main toolbar.

● Messenger always gives you a second chance to change your mind about deleting a message—if you use the Delete button on the main toolbar to "trash" a message, Messenger refiles it into the Trash folder. To truly and permanently throw a message away, you must open the Trash folder, highlight the message you want to get rid of, and click the Delete button again.

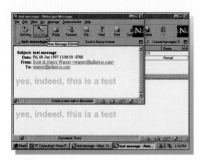

2 Click the New Msg button on the main toolbar and a Message Composition window will appear. Now click the Quote button, and the text of the first message will appear in the body of the new one you're creating.

3 Press Enter once to put some space between the quote and the first line of your new message, and type **Thanks for the e-mail.** Click once in the To: line and add your own e-mail address again, and type **test message 2** in the Subject line. Click the Send button to send it on its way.

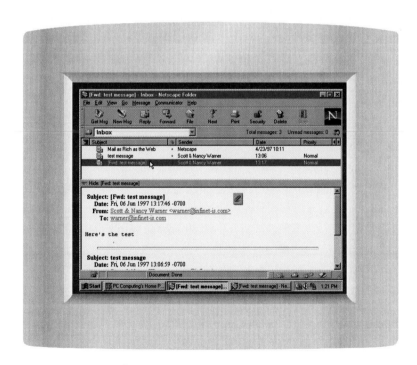

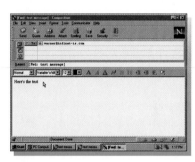

4 You're back where you began, with just your original test message. Now click the Forward button on the main toolbar, and another Message Composition window appears. The Subject line reads "Fwd: test message." You type your e-mail address in the To: line and **Here's the test** in the body. Send this one off, too, by clicking the Send button.

5 Close the original test message by pressing Ctrl+W to get back to the Inbox. Click the Get Mail button to download the messages you just sent to yourself, and let's have a look.

How to Send Attachments

A common use for e-mail is sending someone an *attachment*, a file you add onto your message before saving it to your outbox. With Messenger, you can attach practically any kind of file to an e-mail message—text, pictures, audio or video files, Web pages, bookmark lists—whatever you need to send to someone quickly and efficiently.

1 After you've launched Navigator and opened your Inbox, click the Compose button on the main toolbar to write a new message.

7 This is what a message with an attachment looks like—a description of the attachment appears in a box, along with a link you can click to open it.

● In this lesson, you'll learn how to attach something to an outgoing e-mail message. You'll use a shareware program to complete the exercise, but remember that the procedure described here will work for *any* kind of attachment.

6 Click the Get Mail button to download the messages you just sent to yourself, and let's have a look. Now Messenger must download the movie from the Internet, so wait another moment or two.

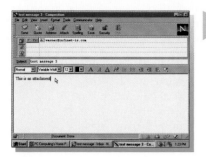

2 Type your own e-mail address in the To: line, **test message 3** in the Subject line, and **This is an attachment** in the body.

3 Now click the Attach button on the main toolbar. You'll find you have several choices on the pull-down menu that pops up. Move the cursor down to File and click once.

4 We're going to attach the tax shareware program you downloaded from Shareware.com. When the Enter File to Attach window appears, find the name of the program and double-click it.

5 Now there's a pathway leading to the movie listed in the Attachment area on the message you're writing. Click the Send button on the main toolbar to complete the task—Messenger has to upload the movie to the Internet so it may take a moment.

How to Use the Address Book

If you're going to send e-mail to a person or group of people on a regular basis, you're going to get tired of typing the same address over and over again. This is why Messenger gives you an address book—so you can make and keep a list of the e-mail addresses you use most often, right at your fingertips for easy access.

1 After you've launched Navigator and accessed Messenger, choose Address Book from the Communicator pull-down menu and click it once.

5 Use the Directory button on the main toolbar to look for an individual's e-mail address, phone number, street address, organization and/or city location. Messenger lets you access Four11's directory or BigFoot's directory, another popular White pages site on the Web.

● **One last piece of "netiquette" advice: don't give people clever, mean, or derogatory nicknames when you list them in your Address Book. It can be tempting and it looks confidential— Messenger provides you with space for nicknames in the New Card window—but some e-mail programs display both the recipient's nickname and real name in the messages you send them. You won't see that nickname in the text of the message you send, but the recipient might.**

2 Click the New Card button on the main toolbar. In the New Card window that comes up, type the first and last name, e-mail address, and any other notes.

3 The Add User window also features a Contact page where you type in an individual's company and job title, their street address, and phone numbers. This information will become useful when you learn to use Netscape Conference in Part 5, so put it in. Click OK when you're finished.

4 If you want to create one address for a group of people—a bowling team, for example—click the New List button. The Mailing List window comes up. This is where you type in all the individual e-mail addresses (press Enter after each one) and give the list a name.

PART 4

Using Collabra: Participating in Newsgroups

IN THIS PART of the book, you'll learn how you can use Netscape Collabra to communicate through Usenet newsgroups. Usenet newsgroups (generally referred to simply as newsgroups) are basically electronic corkboards where anyone can post and read notes related to a unique topic. There are tens of thousands of newsgroups; whatever you're interested in, there's probably a newsgroup about it.

IN THIS SECTION YOU'LL LEARN

How to Use Collabra's Main Toolbar

Like Navigator, Composer, and Messenger, Netscape Collabra provides you with a main toolbar that you can use to perform many basic newsgroup-related tasks. Begin by launching Collabra using the Discussions button on the Component Bar, located in the lower-right corner of Navigator's main window. This opens the Message Center, which you glimpsed in the last part of the book regarding Messenger.

1 The Get Msg button retrieves new, unread messages that have been posted to the newsgroup since your last download.

5 The Stop button works just like it does in Navigator and Messenger: If you change your mind in mid-download, this button will interrupt the incoming file.

● There are many ways of issuing commands in Collabra, just as there are in the other components of Netscape Communicator. If you're a mouse user, use the tools and toolbar. If you prefer menus, use the pull-down menus along the top of the window. And if you're keyboard oriented, there are numerous keyboard shortcuts to help you perform basic newsgroup tasks.

2 The New Msg button enables you to write and post a new message to a newsgroup.

3 The New Folder button creates a new folder in your Inbox, for either newsgroup postings or for e-mail.

4 The Subscribe button subscribes you to a newsgroup—you'll learn more about subscribing later on in this part of the book.

How to Use Collabra's Other Tools

There are other useful tool buttons scattered around the Message Center, and this lesson shows you where they are and how to use them.

Thumbtab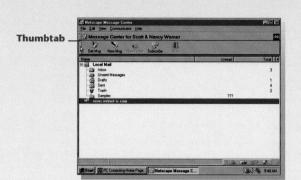

1 As in Navigator, Messenger, and other Communicator components with toolbars, you can switch the position of Collabra's Navigation and Location toolbars by dragging the thumbtabs on the left side.

8 The open/close tab to the left of the Component bar alternatively docks or floats this bar to or from the open window. Clicking the tab in either spot moves this toolbar to the other position.

7 The Navigator button automatically opens a new browser window in Navigator.

● Remember, you can always look at the status bar towards the lower-left corner of Messenger's window if you want a short description of a tool or button. Roll the cursor over the button in question, and its description appears in the status bar.

2 The big *N* or Netscape button will always return you to Netscape's home page, even if you change your default home page to something else (as we did in Part 1).

3 The Message Center columns detail many kinds of information about the messages in your Inbox: subject, sender, date received, priority, status, message length, and more. Clicking each individual button resorts your messages accordingly, and the arrow buttons on the right end of the toolbar allow you to see as many or as few of these categories as you like.

4 The Composer button—on the Component bar—opens Composer. You'll learn more about building Web pages in Part 6.

5 The Discussion Groups button is what took you to the Message Center in the first place.

6 The Mailbox button takes you to where you use Messenger to create, send, and manage e-mail.

How to Use Collabra's File Menu

Collabra's File menu allows you to open browser windows and Web pages; to close, save, and compose newsgroup messages; to work with folders; and to print newsgroup postings.

1 To open the File menu, go to the top of a Collabra newsgroup window, click File, and roll the cursor down the menu to choose from the available options.

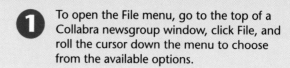

7 Close closes the Message Center, and Exit lets you leave Messenger and Navigator and close all open windows.

6 Send Unsent Messages and Update Message Count, in turn, mail your messages and resort your existing messages. We'll look at Subscribe to Discussion Groups later on in this part of the book. Go Offline lets you disconnect from the Internet while reading and sorting your e-mail and newsgroup postings.

● **The Message Center is the heart of both Messenger and Collabra, as it is where you store, sort, and otherwise manage all your e-mail and newsgroup postings.**

Na_vigator Window   Ctrl+N
_Message   Ctrl+M

Blank _Page   Ctrl+Shift+N
Page From _Template
Page From _Wizard...

2 Selecting New gives you access to several other options: Navigator Window, which opens a blank window in Navigator; Message, which opens a blank e-mail form; and Blank Page, Page From Template, and Page From Wizard, three Web page authoring choices.

Ne_w Discussion Group
New Discussion _Group Server...
_Open Discussion Group   Ctrl+O

3 New Discussion Group, New Discussion Group Server, and Open Discussion Group are features you'll explore later on in this part of the book.

_Rename Folder...
Empt_y Trash Folder
Compress Fol_ders

4 Rename Folder, Empty Trash Folder, and Compress Folders allow you to create a new folder, to empty your Trash, and to squeeze several folders into one, respectively.

_File	_Edit	_View	_Communicator	_Help

_New   ▶
Ne_w Discussion Group
New Discussion _Group Server...
_Open Discussion Group   Ctrl+O

_Rename Folder...
Empt_y Trash Folder
Compress Fol_ders

Ge_t Messages   ▶
Send Unsent Messages
_Update Message Count
Su_bscribe to Discussion Groups...

Go Off_line...

_Close   Ctrl+W
E_xit   Ctrl+Q

5 Get Messages logs you back onto the Internet to retrieve more mail.

How to Use Collabra's Edit Menu

The Edit menu enables you to make various changes to your newgroup postings, such as cutting, copying, and pasting text, as well as undoing and redoing certain edits or commands. You also use the Edit menu options to search newsgroup postings and your Phone book, select groups of postings based on threads and topics, and more. To use the Edit menu, go to the top of a Collabra newsgroup window, click on Edit, and roll the cursor down the menu to choose from the available options.

1 Undo, Redo, Cut, Copy, and Paste all permit you to work with highlighted sections of text in a newsgroup posting.

● As with previous pull-down menus in both Navigator and in Messenger, some menu options are highlighted or usable, and others are unhighlighted or not usable. Which options are available constantly changes as you read, sort, delete, decode, and browse through your different kinds of e-mail. Just remember that Messenger provides you with all the menu options you need as you go.

 Discussion Group Server Properties lets you view information about a Web page's server (not very useful at this point). Preferences, as you may remember, lets you establish or change different mail and group settings.

Delete Discussion Group Server
Select All   Ctrl+A

2 Delete Discussion Group Server effectively unsubscribes you from a newsgroup. Select All lets you select everything in the current window.

Search Messages
Search Directory

3 Search Messages and Search Directory let you search a group of postings as you would search an index: by keyword or phrase.

Manage Mail Account
Manage Discussion Group

4 Manage Mail Account and Manage Discussion Group let you, well, manage your e-mail and newsgroup postings, chiefly by logging on for more postings.

5 The Mail Filters option lets you choose how to sort newsgroup postings as they're downloaded. You can establish new filters and delete or edit existing filters, so all postings regarding one subject are grouped together.

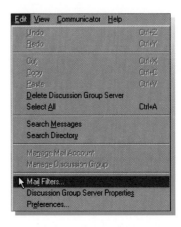

How to Use Collabra's View Menu

Collabra's View menu controls all the ways you look at newsgroup postings and your newsgroup window; think of it as a short, just-the-facts list of how to manage all newsgroup postings. You use the View menu options to sort and unscramble newsgroup postings; to customize window and toolbar display; to load, reload, and update your postings list; and more. To use the View menu, go to the top of a Collabra newsgroup window, click View, and roll the cursor down the menu to choose from the available options.

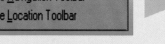

1 Hide/Show Navigation Toolbar and Hide/Show Location Toolbar allow you to hide or reveal these toolbars if you choose. (Here, the menu says "Hide" because the toolbars are visible. If the toolbars were not visible, then the menu would say "Show.")

● Again, if you notice that some of the menu commands are unavailable, that just means that you don't have the appropriate data to work with. Collabra provides you with all the menu options you need as you go.

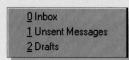

2 Move Folder's submenu lets you move a whole folderful of messages or newsgroup postings to a number of places in the Message Center: Inbox, Unsent Messages, or Drafts...

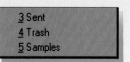

3 ...and/or Sent, Trash, or Samples.

4 Stop Loading works like the Stop button on the main toolbar: It interrupts a current download or newsgroup session.

5 Think of the View menu as a short just-the-facts list of how to manage all newsgroup postings.

How to Use Collabra's Communicator Menu

The Communicator menu in Netscape Collabra is virtually the same as the Communicator menu in Navigator: It helps you easily move among the five parts of Communicator (Navigator, Messenger, Composer, Collabra, and Conference).

1 To open the Communicator menu, click on Communicator and roll the cursor down to choose from the available options.

8 Java Console is an advanced Web page building feature that you may use if you become an advanced Web page designer.

7 History provides a detailed, more technical list of all the sites you've visited during your current session. For now, you may feel satisfied with the list at the end of this menu, which is close to the same thing.

● At the bottom of the menu you'll see a list of all the Web pages you've visited during your current session, numbered in chronological order. Here, you've only been one place, so you only have one location.

2 Selecting the Navigator option opens a new Navigator window. Messenger Mailbox opens your e-mail; Collabra Discussion Groups opens your newsgroup postings; Page Composer opens a blank Web page; and Conference launches Communicator's long-distance calling program.

3 Show/Dock Component Bar determines the location of the button bar in the lower-right corner of Navigator's window. In the central figure in this section, it's "docked," but here it's "shown."

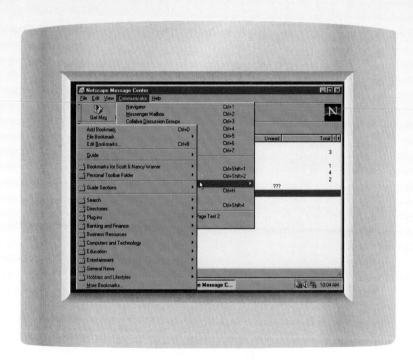

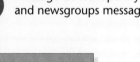

4 Message Center opens your e-mail and newsgroups message center.

5 Address Book is a list of e-mail addresses and newsgroups you write to frequently; see Part 3 for more information about how to set it up.

6 Bookmarks provides a way to store URLs or addresses of Web pages you want to visit many times. (You learned about bookmarks in Part 2.)

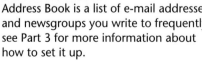

How to Use Collabra's Help Menu

The Help menu is one of Collabra's best features for the new user. This section explores all the Help menu items in detail.

1 To open the Help menu, click on the word Help at the top of Collabra's window.

8 About Communicator, the last item on the Help menu, is some legal jargon that you may or may not want to read. Either way, you've finished looking at the Help menu and the entire set of pull-down menus. Now you're on your way.

7 About Font Displayers touches on questions concerning dynamic text and other, similar subjects.

Help Contents   F1
Release Notes
Product Information and Support

2 If you want to read about Navigator's various features and capabilities, select Help Contents, Release Notes, and/or Product Information and Support. We will explore how to use Help Contents, or NetHelp, in one of the Projects at the end of the book.

Software Updates
Register Now
Member Services

3 We already checked out Software Updates and Register Now in Part 1, and Member Services contains the same type of information.

4 International Users contains specific information about using Communicator with languages other than English and in countries outside the United States.

Security
Net Etiquette

5 Security is covered in depth in Part 7, along with other issues. Net Etiquette provides newcomers to the Internet with an outline of basic online manners.

6 About Plug-ins opens a list of audio, video, and other multimedia components already installed on your computer with Navigator.

How to Find and Subscribe to Newsgroups

Y ou already set up your newsgroup reader using the Mail and News Wizard, so now you can jump on into the world of Collabra, Netscape's newsgroup program. In this section, you learn how to find newsgroups that fit your particular interests and how to subscribe to them. First launch Navigator and then access Collabra through the Component bar in the lower-right corner of Navigator's window. The Message Center opens, displaying both your e-mail and newsgroup folders.

1 After you've launched Navigator and accessed Collabra, click once on the news folder to highlight it—on the desktop shown here, it's called news.infinet-is.com. Now open the File menu and select Subscribe to Discussion Groups.

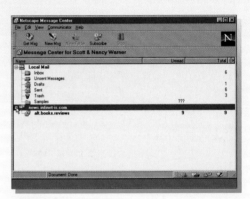

7 Now when you open your newsgroup folder, it will reveal your new subscription.

● The alt collection of newsgroups has gotten lots of bad press, some of it deserved but mostly not. Some alt newsgroups concern subjects that are graphic, sexual, and, for some people, objectionable. Usually, if you want to know what its subscribers are discussing, you can almost always figure it out from the newsgroup name.

● If you're using Collabra from a computer in your office, check with your systems administrator before you subscribe to any newsgroups. Because of the nature of some newsgroup discussions, many businesses forbid their employees to use company computers for newsgroup subscription.

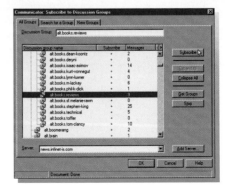

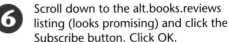

6 Scroll down to the alt.books.reviews listing (looks promising) and click the Subscribe button. Click OK.

2 Now you're looking at the Subscribe to Discussion Groups window. Collabra will automatically begin retrieving the full list of newsgroups. This may take a few moments—there's a lot of newsgroups out there—so have a little patience.

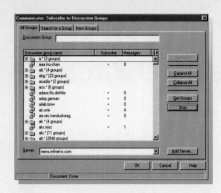

3 Here's the entire list of all the newsgroups in existence—pretty daunting, isn't it? For the purposes of this exercise, we're going to work with one or two newsgroups, but if you decide you really like newsgroups and want to jump in with both feet, you should take some time and look through the entire list.

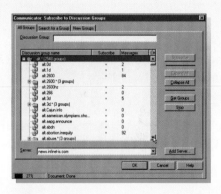

4 Find and open the alt folder by clicking the entry once and clicking the plus sign to the left of the folder icon. A second set of folders will appear. This is the list of newsgroups you want to search; use the scroll bar by clicking the down arrow and holding down your mouse key.

5 Looking for something to read? There are two entries entitled alt.books on the list: an individual newsgroup indicated by the tiny newspaper icon, and a folder of newsgroups with *alt.books* in the title. Click the plus sign to the left of the alt.books folder to look at all the options.

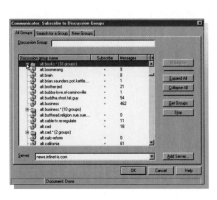

How to Read and Write Newsgroup Postings

Now that you've subscribed to a newsgroup, you can join in on the discussion. In this lesson, you learn how to download and read newsgroup postings using Collabra and the Message Center.

1 After launching Navigator and accessing Collabra through the Component bar, click on the plus sign to the left of your main newsgroup folder (the one shown here is called news.infinet-is.com) to open it.

7 When you're finished reading, click the Message Center button to return to the main newsgroup window.

● Your Internet service provider (ISP) may have special policies and/or user options for newsgroups that you may find interesting. Some ISPs allow subscribers to block certain kinds of newsgroups (with alt.sex in the name, for example), or they can provide subscribers with password protection. Contact your ISP and ask if they offer such features for your account.

● Collabra allows you to use different fonts, styles, colors, and other stylistic tools when you create newsgroup postings.

6 If you want to write a new post, click the New Message button on the main toolbar. Another new posting window opens; write your message (don't forget the subject line) and click Send when you're finished.

2 Double-click on alt.books.reviews. A new window appears, listing all the individual postings in the newsgroup. Collabra automatically brings you to the top of the list; double-click on a message to open it. If you get to the end or you want to check for new postings, click the Get Msg button on the main toolbar.

3 This is what a newsgroup posting (or article) looks like. Once you're done reading, click the Next button on the main toolbar to browse through the remaining messages.

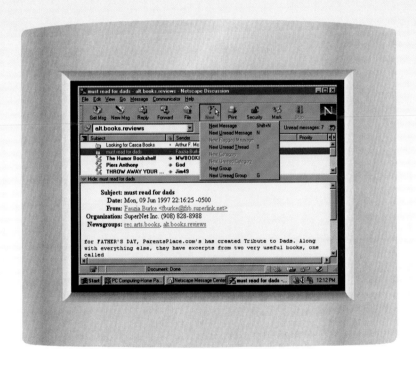

4 When you want to respond to a particular post, click the Reply button on the main toolbar. This button gives you four options: Reply to Sender is for the posting author only; Reply to Sender and All Recipients is for the author and everyone who replied; Reply to Group posts to all subscribers; and Reply to Sender and Group posts to everyone in the group and the author. Click Reply to Sender.

5 The window that opens looks and works very much like the window you use to write an e-mail message. One of the differences, of course, is the name of the newsgroup in the address window. Type your reply and click the Send button when you're finished.

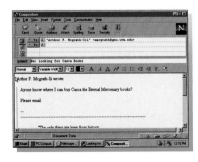

How to Add and Delete Newsgroups

There are times when you'll want to join a newsgroup whose name you already know, because a friend recommended it, for instance. And sometimes you'll want to leave or unsubscribe from a newsgroup if the conversation isn't the style you like or if the topics of discussion don't interest you. This lesson shows you how to handle both situations.

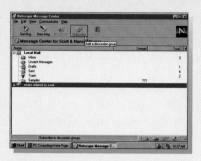

1 After accessing Collabra, click the Subscribe button on the main toolbar.

5 Now you're back where you started, without Tom Clancy.

● Remember that your Internet service provider may be able to keep certain newsgroups from coming into your account, either because of provisions of your specific account or because of a company content policy. If someone who uses your account keeps subscribing to newsgroups you find objectionable, don't keep playing the unsubscribe game. Call your ISP and see if they can help you.

2 A window appears with a space at the top for you to type in the name of the newsgroup you want to join. Type in **alt.books.tom-clancy** and click Subscribe.

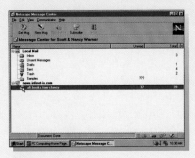

3 There's your new newsgroup listing, right where it should be. Double-click on it to download the postings and read what's going on.

4 Not quite what you had in mind? Close the alt.books.tom-clancy window to return to where you started. Click the listing for alt.books.tom-clancy and click Unsubscribe. A warning dialog box will pop up and ask if you really want to unsubscribe—click OK.

P A R T   5

Using Conference: Placing Long Distance Calls over the Internet

YOU'RE about to discover the best-kept secret of the Internet: By using software like Netscape Conference, you can make real-time long distance phone calls for nothing more than the cost of your Internet account.

In this part of the book, you'll learn the basics of Conference by getting familiar with its toolbars and pull-down menus. You'll prepare to make and receive long distance calls; establish a phone book and speed dial numbers; use Conference's collaborative whiteboard and chat tool; and more.

IN THIS SECTION YOU'LL LEARN

How to Use Conference's Toolbar and Other Buttons

Netscape Conference may not look quite the same as Collabra, Composer, Navigator, and Messenger, but you still find your way around via toolbar buttons and pull-down menus. To get started, launch Navigator and log onto the Internet. Open the Communicator pull-down menu, choose Conference, and click once. Now you're on your way.

1 The Whiteboard button on the main toolbar takes you to Conference's shared whiteboard—like the one in your employer's actual meeting room—where you can write with different colored "markers," type text, or sketch out your ideas.

9 If you want to record a Conference call, you'd use the Microphone button. Use the Speakers button to play back what you taped.

8 When you click the Mode button, some legal and technical information about Netscape appears, much as it does when you use the Help pull-down menus in Collabra, Messenger, and Composer.

2 The Collaborative Browsing button allows you to direct one or more other people to different Web sites via Navigator. If you're the "leader," all the other people in your group can watch your progress in their Navigator window as you surf around the Web.

3 The File Exchange button enables you to trade a file on your computer with someone else while you are both using Conference.

4 The Chat button opens up the Chat Tool, where you and other people you're calling can jot notes on a Personal Note Pad; cut, paste, and otherwise edit your thoughts; and send Notes to another person.

5 Use the Dial button to place a call after you've typed in the e-mail or netphone address of the person you want to contact.

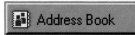

7 The Address Book button opens the list of e-mail addresses you learned about in Part 3. You can place a call via Conference using either an e-mail address or a netphone number.

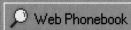

6 The Web Phonebook button takes you to Netscape's online Directory, where Communicator users who've registered Conference are listed with their netphone numbers (you'll learn how to set up Conference in Part 5).

How to Use Conference's Pull-Down Menus

Conference's various features and capabilities are presented to you on two groups of pull-down menus. There are three pull-down menus along the top of Conference's window, and two open/close-tabbed menus within. Since there are not always keyboard shortcuts or buttons for these menu items, you'll get an extended introduction to the pull-down menus in the next four pages.

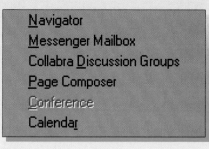

1 The first two items on the Call pull-down menu are Dial and Hang Up—quite self-explanatory. When you're off the phone, Hang Up is shaded and unusable, and when you're in the middle of a call, Dial is shaded and unusable.

8 The top portion of the Communicator pull-down menu resembles all the other Communicator menus, with links to Navigator, Messenger, Collabra, Composer, Conference, and to Calendar (a feature of the Professional edition).

7 The SpeedDial menu will eventually become a short list of memorized numbers that you call most often.

● See the inside front cover of the book for keyboard shortcuts for some of Conference's basic functions.

2 Direct Call lets you type in a person's netphone number or e-mail address with a minimum number of steps to go through or buttons to push.

3 Always Prompt is like having a secretary—if someone is trying to call you, they must wait to see if you answer Conference's prompt first. Auto Answer, on the other hand, lets people connect to you directly. And Do Not Disturb rejects all incoming calls—notice when you click this Call menu option once, the Mode button changes to let you know you won't be receiving incoming calls.

4 Show/Hide Window alternatively conceals and reveals the Conference window while you are connected.

5 The Call Log keeps track of calls you place and calls you receive, in case you like to keep track of this kind of information, too. You'll establish your Preferences later on in this part, so remember where this menu option is.

6 Exit is also pretty self-explanatory. Just remember that this is the way you quit and shut down Conference entirely—don't use it, for example, to hang up or end a phone call.

How to Use Conference's Pull-Down Menus (Continued)

9 The SpeedDial menu will eventually become a short list of memorized numbers you call most often. Right now, though, you haven't learned how to assign SpeedDial numbers, so all six numbers are shaded and unusable.

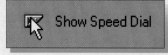

15 There's one more "pull-down" menu in the middle of Conference's window—the tab named Show/Hide Speed Dial. If you click it once, the Conference window enlarges to show six Speed Dial buttons you can use in lieu of the SpeedDial pull-down menu if you prefer.

14 About Netscape Conference and About Communicator contain legal jargon mostly (only) of interest to lawyers.

10 The Address Book and Web Phonebook help you quickly locate people you wish to contact. Voice Mail lets you leave the online equivalent of an answering message (this is covered in detail later on in this section of the book).

Address Book
Web Phonebook
Voice Mail

Whiteboard
Collaborative Browsing
File Exchange
Chat

11 The last portion of the Communicator menu repeats the options presented by the four buttons on the main Toolbar: Whiteboard, Collaborative Browsing, File Exchange, and Chat.

Help Contents
Release Notes
Frequently Asked Questions

12 On the Help menu, Help Contents directs you to NetHelp, Netscape's keyword-searchable help directory you'll learn to use in a Project later on. Release Notes lists bugs, problems, and other technical topics about Communicator. Frequently Asked Questions is really a list of frequently sought answers.

13 The Setup Wizard is how you set up Conference to get started, and Troubleshooting Audio helps you fine-tune Conference during a phone call.

Setup Wizard...
Troubleshooting Audio

How to Establish Conference Preferences

Customizing any software component or program means choosing some of the features you do and don't want activated, indicating the way you want the software to run, and specifying what kind of Internet connection you're using while you run it. Conference Preferences are no different, so get ready to tailor Conference to your own personal needs and preferences.

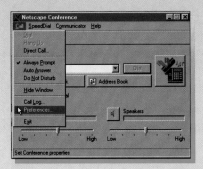

1 First, open the Call pull-down menu and choose Preferences. This brings up the Preferences dialog box.

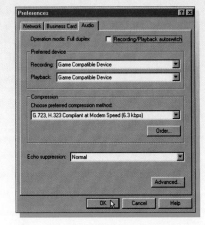

5 Finally, click the Audio "page" tab once to open your Audio preferences. Unless you're a multimedia specialist or an otherwise sound-savvy professional, don't change these presets. Just remember that this is the area in your Preferences file you may have to change later if you experience sound quality problems.

● Unfortunately, in the time it took to write this part (roughly two hours) I received 18 unsolicited Conference calls from 18 different callers, all with male names or aliases. A random sampling of these calls revealed sexually suggestive or explicit content, so female users and parents with young children may wish to permanently leave the Always Prompt or even the Do Not Disturb option checked on the Call pull-down menu.

2 Network, the first "page" of your Conference Preferences, establishes some calling basics. The DLS server, netdls.four11.com, is a preset that you should not change. However, remember the checkbox below it that reads "List my name in phonebook," even though you should leave it checked for now.

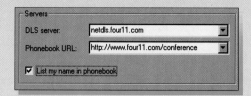

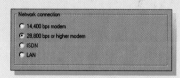

3 Network Connection is another no-brainer. If you have a connection slower than 14.4Kbps, though, Conference may not work for you at all and there's nothing here you can do to change that.

4 Now click the Business Card "page" once to open your Business Card preferences. The information you type in here will be displayed to everyone with access to Netscape's online directory, so choose wisely. You also may or may not wish to display a picture of yourself— you'll learn how to do this in a Project so you have some time to think about it.

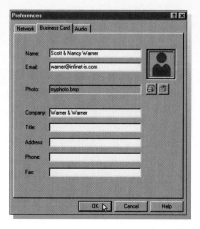

How to Use the Microphone and Speakers

Conference is the only part of the Communicator suite that requires you to have additional hardware. As already mentioned, in order to send and receive Conference calls you must have a set of external speakers and a microphone in addition to your monitor, keyboard, and computer. Luckily, many Windows machines come with this extra hardware, but Conference still requires you to learn how to use it.

1 This exercise will familiarize you with the lower portion of Conference's window, where the Microphone and Speakers controls are featured.

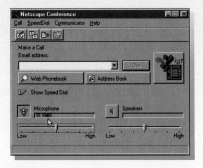

6 Click and drag the red dot to the right until it's in synch with the volume of your voice. In this example, the setting is just right.

● Before you get into the next chapter, make sure your microphone and speakers are properly plugged in and that the plugs are firmly seated. This isn't directly related to using Conference, but if your plugs are loose in their sockets, you won't be communicating very well.

● Don't expect Conference to deliver "pin-drop" sound quality—high traffic volume, connection speed, geographical distance and background noise can all affect the clarity of your Conference long distance phone call. If you get a bad connection, all you can do is hang up and try again.

2 You can use the Record Audio button to record a Conference call. This will activate the microphone meter/sliding adjuster bar next to it.

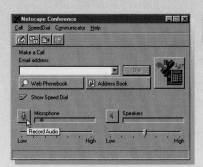

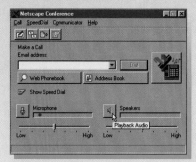

3 The Speakers button plays back any recorded audio, but the meter/sliding adjuster next to it measures the volume of your caller's voice.

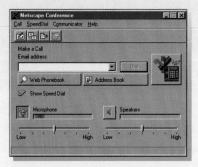

4 This is what the Speakers level meter looks like when the setting is properly established.

5 You should also experiment with the slider in the Microphone meter. If you set it too low, your caller won't be able to hear you—but if you set it too high, your caller will be able to hear your dog barking, your television blaring, and your kids yelling along with (or instead of) your voice. In this example, the Microphone Level is set too low.

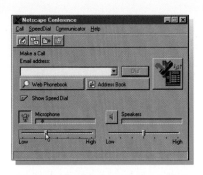

How to Set Up Conference: The Setup Wizard

In this section, you'll use Conference's Setup Wizard to establish a Business Card, to verify your modem and processor speed; and to run a test of your system to make sure you have the power to operate Conference.

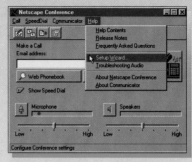

1 Launch Communicator and log onto the Internet. Choose Conference from Navigator's Communicator pull-down menu, and then choose Setup Wizard from Conference's Help pull-down menu.

8 Click Finish to complete setup and exit the Wizard. Communicator will now automatically launch Conference, and you don't need to restart your computer to get started.

7 Now Conference will test your computer to see if you can run it successfully. Did you pass? Congratulations!

● Keep in mind when setting up your Business Card that the information you give will be revealed to anyone who calls you—not just people that you call. It may be most prudent to limit your Business Card information to your name and e-mail address, leaving off your street address and phone number, especially if you have concerns about security.

2 Read the first two windows of preliminary instructions and click Next each time you're finished. Click Next once more to go forward with the setup process.

3 Here's the Business Card page, where you can provide Conference with lots of identifying information about yourself (including your picture) though remember, it will all be posted to the Internet. Click next after you've typed in your name and e-mail address.

4 Conference will show you your DLS server name and the phonebook URL. Leave these settings as they are shown, and leave yourself listed on Netscape's phonebook, too. Then click Next.

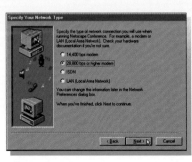

5 Now choose the type of modem or Internet connection you're using and click Next.

6 Conference will now identify your sound card(s). These settings are also fine, so click Next.

How to Place a Call Using an E-mail Address

When you use a regular telephone, you either dial a number you know or you pause to look up a new number using some kind of listing. In this exercise, you're going to use Conference to contact an individual you know using his or her e-mail address. Later on, you'll learn more about where to find actual Conference phone numbers, and how to customize Conference's speed dial functions.

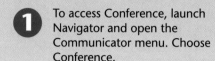

1 To access Conference, launch Navigator and open the Communicator menu. Choose Conference.

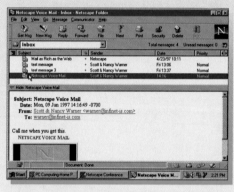

7 Now let's check your voice mail: it's saved in Messenger's Mailbox along with your other unread e-mail. Choose Messenger from the Communicator pull-down menu; then click the Get Msg button; and you'll find your voice mail message. Double-click to read it.

 FYI

● If you are trying to call someone using their CompuServe, America Online, or other specific online service address, you won't be able to talk to them with Conference. This would be like trying to call someone who doesn't have a telephone—the person you're calling also has to have Communicator installed. You can leave "voice-mail" in such a person's mailbox, but they won't be able to call you back.

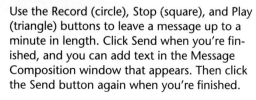

6 Use the Record (circle), Stop (square), and Play (triangle) buttons to leave a message up to a minute in length. Click Send when you're finished, and you can add text in the Message Composition window that appears. Then click the Send button again when you're finished.

2 Click the E-mail Address location window once to activate the cursor, then type in the e-mail address of the person you want to call. Then click the Dial button.

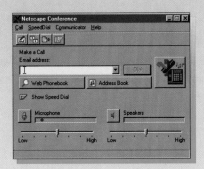

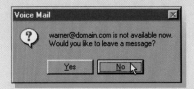

3 Conference will try to place the call, but if the person doesn't answer you will get an "unavailable" response. Click Yes to leave voice mail, or click No to abort the call. For now, click No.

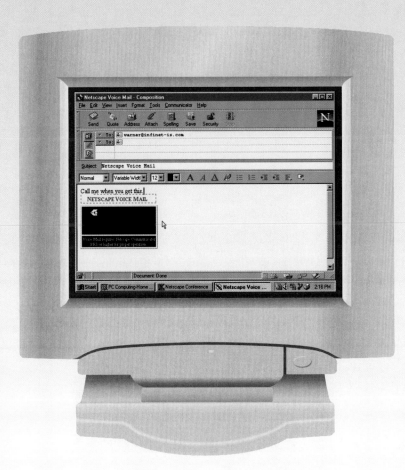

4 Conference will always tell you the status of a call you're making via this Pending Invitation dialog box. "Failed to connect" can mean any number of things—perhaps the e-mail account is inactive, the person you're calling doesn't have Communicator installed, or something else.

5 Now try to call yourself—type your own e-mail address in the E-mail Address location box—and this time click Yes when Conference asks if you want to leave voice mail.

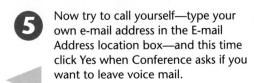

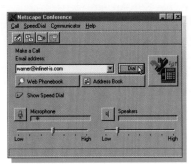

How to Place a Call Using a Web Phonebook Number

When you used Conference's Setup Wizard to get started with this part of the book, you automatically established a listing for yourself on Netscape Conference's Web Phonebook, an area on Netscape's Web site that's a lot like Four11. In this exercise, you learn how to place a call to someone after finding their listing on Netscape's Web Phonebook.

● It's possible that if you and the person you're calling have very different modem speeds—if he or she has an ISDN line and you have a 28.8Kbps modem, for example—there will be a significant time lag. If you have audio difficulties, use the Chat tool or the Whiteboard instead.

● Netscape's Conference phone book lists people alphabetically by the first name entered in the Business Card name space. So if you want your listing to come under the first letter of your last name, list yourself as Doe John rather than John Doe.

1 To access Conference, launch Navigator and open the Communicator menu. Choose Conference.

7 Click the Hang Up button to disconnect the call, or choose Hang Up from the Call pull-down menu. The Drop Call dialog box will appear, asking if you're sure you want to end the call. Click Yes once, and your call is ended.

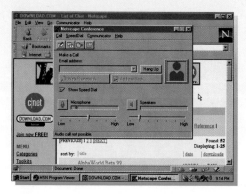

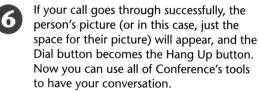

6 If your call goes through successfully, the person's picture (or in this case, just the space for their picture) will appear, and the Dial button becomes the Hang Up button. Now you can use all of Conference's tools to have your conversation.

2 From the main Conference window, click Web Phonebook once. This will bring up a Navigator browser window and give you access to Netscape's Conference Web Phonebook page on Netscape's Web site.

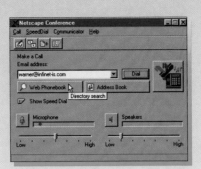

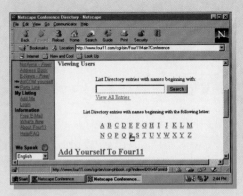

3 In the right frame there's an alphabetical listing of Conference entries. For purposes of this exercise, double-click the R listing.

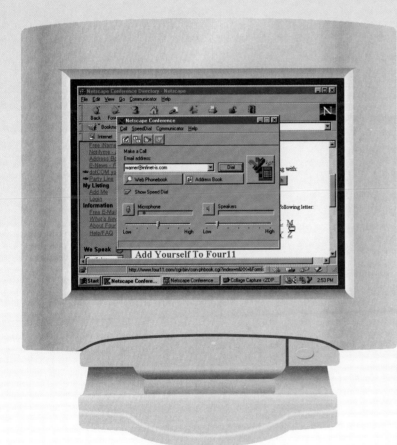

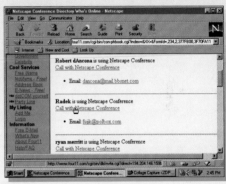

4 Click the person's name—which is also the link to his or her Conference number—once. The Conference main window will appear with a netphone number highlighted in the Location box. This is the "phone number" equivalent to the person's e-mail address.

5 Conference will show you the Pending Invitation dialog box, letting you know the line is ringing.

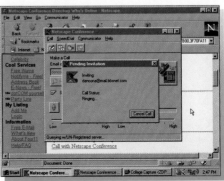

How to Save, Edit, and Delete a Speed Dial Number

If there's a particular number (or numbers) you call often, you may want to use Conference's Speed Dial capability. You can store up to six numbers on a speed dial feature on Conference's main window, just as you can store numbers on a regular telephone list.

1 To access Conference, launch Navigator and open the Communicator menu. Choose Conference.

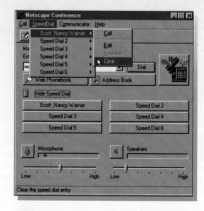

6 To edit or delete your speed dial menu, open the SpeedDial pull-down menu and let the cursor rest on the related entry button. A sub-menu will appear with Edit, Replace, and/or Clear options.

• You can also save Conference netphone numbers in your Address Book, so you don't necessarily have to save a number to Speed Dial if you already have the person listed.

2 To save a number to Conference's Speed Dial feature, first open the Speed Dial pull-down menu in the middle of the window. Click once on the Show/Hide Speed Dial button.

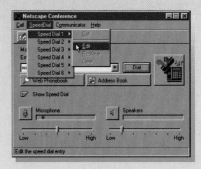

3 Click the first button—Speed Dial 1—to establish its number. Because there is no number in there at present, the menu offers you only the Edit function so that you can establish one.

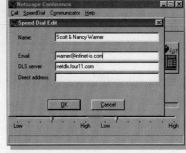

4 Type the person's real name, e-mail address, and his or her Conference netphone number (if different) in the boxes provided in the Speed Dial Edit dialog box and click OK.

5 Now you return to Conference's main window, and the person's real name has replaced the Speed Dial 1 label.

How to Use the Shared Whiteboard

If you're in the middle of a Conference call and you want to visually illustrate your point, Conference gives you the option of using the Whiteboard. This whiteboard is a virtual version of the writing surface hanging on the wall of almost every real conference hall and meeting room, complete with color markers.

1 To access Conference, launch Navigator and open the Communicator menu. Choose Conference.

7 When you're completely finished, even if you're not done with your call, choose Close from the File pull-down menu to close the Whiteboard.

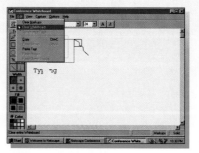

6 To clear the entire Whiteboard, open the Edit pull-down menu and choose Clear Whiteboard.

● Don't forget to explore the rest of the Whiteboard's features—there's plenty more to explore.

2 After you have placed your Conference call, click the Whiteboard button on the main tool-bar. The Whiteboard window will appear.

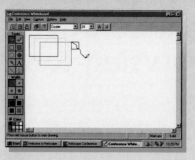

3 You have many writing options: you can write freehand, draw shapes, and select different colors, just to name a few. (It helps to assign each person a different color if many people are using the Board.)

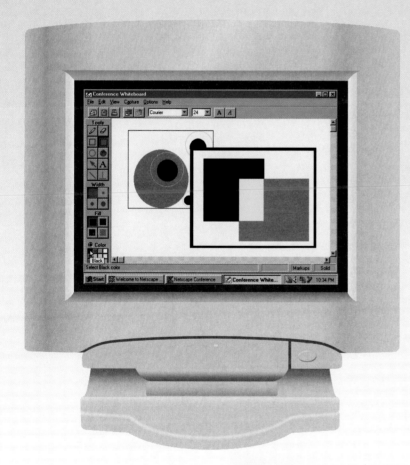

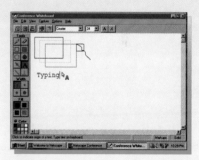

4 You also have several typing options. Click once on a color in the color menu, click the Type tool (the capital A) and click a blank spot on the Board to type your message. Again, different people can use different colors.

5 To erase something, click the Eraser tool and move it over the Board while holding the mouse key down. If you just need more room, use the scroll bar to roll up some new, blank space.

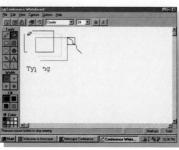

How to Use the Collaborative Browsing Tool

Conference's Collaborative Browsing tool allows two people to surf the Web together, so that you can show each other sites of mutual interest.

1 To access Conference, launch Navigator and open the Communicator menu. Choose Conference.

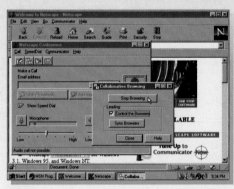

7 When you're finished, click the Stop Browsing/Close button once. Now you can continue with your call, use another tool, or hang up.

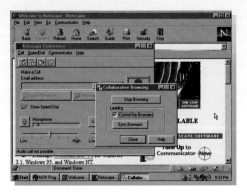

● You may experience difficulty browsing in sync if you and the other caller have different connections or modem speeds.

6 The Sync Browsers button enables the leader to move both browsers to a new Web page at the same time.

2 Once your call has been placed, click the Collaborative Browsing button on the main toolbar. The Collaborative Browsing dialog box will appear.

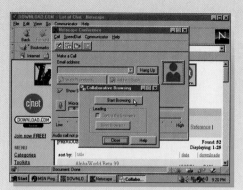

3 Click once on the Start Browsing buttonBrowsing button—you are now "in the lead," deciding where you and the other caller should go.

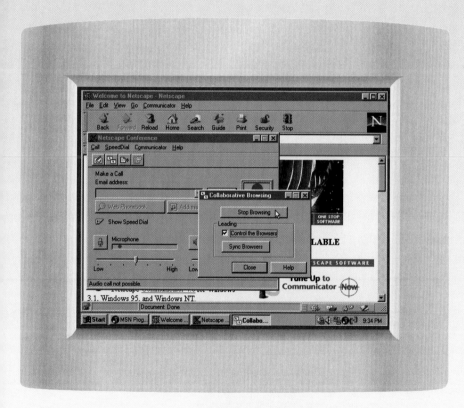

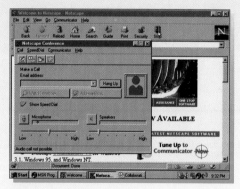

4 From this point forward, you and the other caller can surf together and speak to each other using Conference.

5 If the other person (not the leader) wants to take control, he or she (or you) should click the Leading button once.

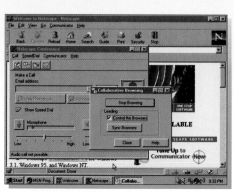

How to Use the File Exchange Tool

The File Exchange tool on Conference's main toolbar lets you distribute a file from your hard drive over the Internet to another person, sort of like handing them a proposal or a memo.

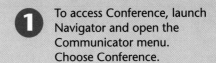

1 To access Conference, launch Navigator and open the Communicator menu. Choose Conference.

8 To close the file-sending tool, choose Close from the File pull-down menu.

7 Choosing Pop Up On Receive from the same pull-down menu will cause the file to automatically open on the receiver's desktop as soon as it has transmitted completely.

● If your connection is slow, it will take a long time for files to be transferred from your computer. The amount of Web traffic may also be a factor, because transferring can take even longer during peak usage times.

2 Once your call has gone through, click the File Exchange button on the main toolbar once.

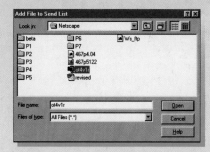

3 The Conference File Exchange window will appear. To select the file you want to send, open the File pull-down menu and choose Add to Send List. The Add File to Send List dialog box will appear—double-click the listing of the file you want to send.

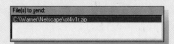

4 The path to the file you want to send will appear in the top window, aptly named File(s) to Send. Click the Send button on the main toolbar to transmit the file.

5 When the person you're calling has received the file, its name will appear in the lower half of the window.

6 If the file you want to send is large and/or confidential, open the Options pull-down window and choose Compress to temporarily shrink the file's size, or choose Ascii or Binary to encode it.

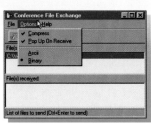

How to Use the Chat Tool

If you prefer to type rather than speak, or if you're having difficulty with your call, the Chat tool is a way to clarify what's going on.

1 To access Conference, launch Navigator and open the Communicator menu. Choose Conference.

8 To end the Chat session without ending the Conference call, choose Close from the File pull-down menu.

● If you'd prefer to choose whether or not you want to participate in a chat session, open the Chat tool Options pull-down menu and uncheck Pop Up On Receive. This will prevent someone from surprising you with an unwanted chat session, the same way Always Prompt prevents unwanted calls.

7 To save a copy of your written conversation, click the Save button on the main toolbar and choose a file name. Communicator will store the conversation on your hard drive.

2 Once your call has connected, click the Chat button on the main toolbar. The Conference Text Chat window will appear.

3 First, type what you want to say into the Personal Note Pad area on the bottom half of the window. Then use the Send button on the main toolbar to submit your comments.

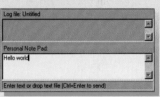

4 What you typed will appear with your name in the upper half of the window, along with the other caller's comments.

5 You can attach a file to your comments by using the Include button on the main toolbar. (See the previous exercise for general information on file transferal.)

6 You can also customize the font, font size, and color of your text display by choosing Font from the Options menu.

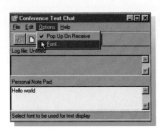

PART 6

Using Composer: Building Your Own Web Pages

IF YOU'VE LONGED to make your own Web pages, then you'll be glad to get to know Netscape Composer, the Web page construction/editing program that's included in Netscape Communicator. More powerful and flexible than Navigator Gold, Composer lets you build your own Web pages from templates or from scratch. Now you have a choice if you want to go it alone.

In this section, you'll become acquainted with Composer's toolbars and menus, which are extremely important. Composer is designed around its menus and tools like the other Communicator components, but there's a lot more to cover. So launch Navigator, log onto the Internet, and click the Editor button on the Component bar to launch Composer.

IN THIS SECTION YOU'LL LEARN

How to Use Composer's Main Toolbar

Composer's main toolbar has many more buttons than the ones in Collabra, Navigator, Messenger, or Conference. From left to right they are New, Open, Save, Publish, Preview, Cut, Copy, Paste, Print, Find, Link, Target, Image, H. Line, Table, and Spelling. See how much there is to explore?

1 New opens a blank Composer window in which you construct a Web page from scratch; Open opens a finished or incomplete Web page you've saved; and Save saves your Web page to your location of choice. You can see that some Composer functions have been designed to resemble word processor features, so you will find them more familiar.

6 Finally, the Spelling button lets you spell check your page before you publish it.

● As with previous pull-down menus in both Navigator and Messenger, some menu options will be highlighted or usable, and others will be unhighlighted or not usable. The menu items available to you change as you read, sort, delete, decode, and browse through your different kinds of e-mail. Just remember that Messenger will provide you with all the menu options you need as you go.

2 You use the Publish button to place your completed Web page on the Internet. Preview lets you see a Web page in Composer, so you can make changes or see how it was constructed.

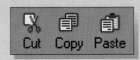

3 Cut, Copy, and Paste are old friends: click and drag the mouse over an element in a Web page to select it, then use Cut to remove it, Copy to duplicate it, and/or Paste to insert it elsewhere.

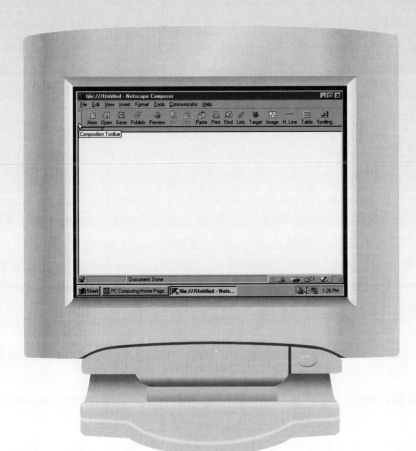

4 Print lets you print a Web page onto paper exactly as you see it on the screen, while Find lets you search a Web page as you would search a document for a specific word, command, or file.

5 There are five Insert buttons on the right end of the main toolbar that help you add elements to your page: Link lets you add a link to another Web page, Target helps you navigate quickly down a long Web page, Image helps you add pictures, H. Line adds dividing lines, and Table lets you arrange many elements within a small, defined area.

How to Use Composer's Format Toolbar

Composer's Format toolbar helps you style, format, and arrange the contents of your Web page: words, links, images, tables, and more. To use the format buttons, first select the text you wish to change on your Web page. Composer will keep the text highlighted while you choose style, color, alignment, and so on.

1 The Paragraph Style drop-down list opens when you click the down arrow. It has 12 options for formatting paragraphs.

8 Finally, the Alignment button actually opens up into three choices: from top to bottom, Align Left (Composer's default), Center, and Align Right.

7 The Decrease Indent and Increase Indent buttons help you quickly create an outline.

● For a comprehensive list of all Communicator's keyboard shortcuts, see the inside back cover of the book.

2 The Font drop-down list also opens with a click of the arrow. Arial, Times, and Courier are all good alternatives to the default font, and the Fixed Width option may become appealing when you get into tables.

3 The Font Size drop-down list lets you increase or decrease the overall size of your text by point size, 8 points being the smallest and 36 points being the largest. You'll get to play with this feature later on in this part of the book.

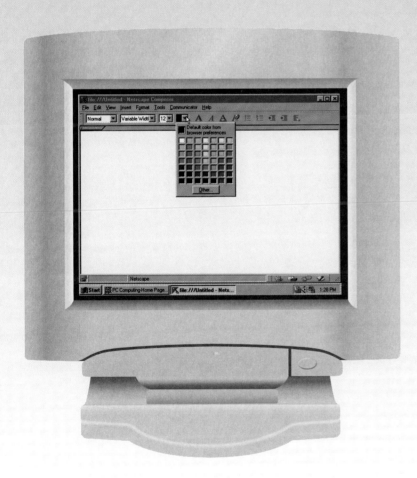

4 Font Color gives you a rainbow of color choices beyond the default black.

5 The next three buttons enable you to apply bold, italic, and underline features, respectively, with a single click of your mouse key.

6 Use the Bullet List and Numbered List buttons to automatically create item lists: Simply type and use the Return key to begin each new item.

How to Use Composer's File Menu

Composer's File menu contains many features found in other File menus you've explored, but there are additional menu items for creating, browsing, and publishing new Web pages.

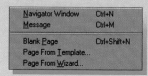

1 The New command opens a submenu that contains Navigator Window, which opens a blank window in Navigator; Message, which opens a blank e-mail form; and Blank Page, Page From Template, and Page From Wizard, three Web page authoring choices.

 6 Close closes Composer without closing Communicator, while Exit is the way to shut down Communicator altogether.

● Many of these commands have keyboard shortcuts. See the inside back cover for a comprehensive list of all Communicator's keyboard shortcuts.

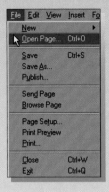

2 The Open Page item works like the Open button on the main toolbar, in that it calls up a Web page already saved to your computer.

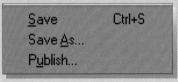

3 Save, naturally, saves what you're creating to your computer after you give it a name, whereas Save As lets you save a duplicate of an open page. Publish uploads a finished Web page to your ISP.

Send Page
Browse Page

4 Send Page lets you e-mail the Web page you're working on via Messenger, while Browse Page lets you view your page in Navigator as it would appear on the Web.

5 Page Setup lets you change printing options like margins, headers, and footers; Print Preview displays the entire page you want to print; and Print works like the Print button on the main toolbar.

Page Setup...
Print Preview
Print...

How to Use Composer's Edit Menu

In addition to common Edit menu features, the Composer Edit menu lets you select and delete tables, remove links, search Web pages for all kinds of elements, view a Web page's source code, and access your preferences.

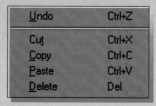

1 Undo lets you take back deletions, insertions, and other changes you make. Cut, Copy, and Paste work exactly like their counterparts on the main toolbar, and Delete erases highlighted text or elements with one click of the mouse.

6 Preferences allows you to revisit your overall preferences, which affect the way you use all the different Communicator components, including Composer. You won't need to set any new preferences to use Composer, however.

● **For a comprehensive list of all Communicator's keyboard shortcuts, see the inside back cover of the book.**

Delete Table   ▶
Remove Link

2 Delete Table and Remove Link are Web page composition options that allow you to get rid of whole elements without messing up the rest of your page. (You're not currently building a page, so these options are not usable.)

Select All   Ctrl+A
Select Table

3 Select All lets you select every element in your Web page, so that you can apply global formatting, copy everything to another document, and so on. Select Table lets you select an entire table.

Find in Page...   Ctrl+F
Find Again   F3
Search Directory

4 Find in Page lets you search a Web page by keyword, Find Again allows you to repeat your last search, and Search Directory brings up the Four11 Search dialog box.

5 HTML Source enables you to view the *source code*, or HTML language, of the Web page you're creating. This is an advanced Composer feature you'll learn more about later on in this section of the book.

How to Use Composer's View Menu

Composer's View menu lets you customize the appearance of Composer's main window and create and establish paragraph marks and tables, and it provides access to advanced Web page design information, such as document information and source code.

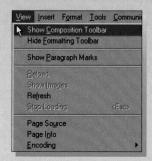

1 Hide/Show Composition Toolbar enables you to conceal the main toolbar if you prefer. Sometimes hiding a toolbar provides that little bit of extra screen space that you need to see all of your project.

7 Encoding, if you recall, is a languages feature you don't need to think about because you want Composer to display text in English.

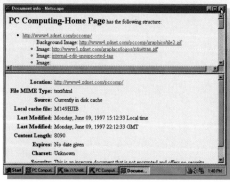

● Remember that if an item on a pull-down menu is hard to read, it's shaded or inactive for a reason: You don't need to or cannot use it at the moment.

6 Here's what selecting Page Info shows you about a Web page: more advanced, general information that doesn't necessarily help you at this early stage.

2 Hide/Show Formatting Toolbar lets you conceal the other toolbar at the top of Composer's window. In this example, both toolbars are hidden, leaving you a little more room to work.

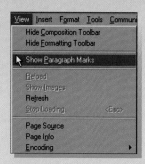

3 Hide/Show Paragraph Marks either shows or hides Composer's paragraph symbol (a small rectangle) at the point where you press Enter to end a line.

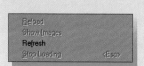

4 Reload and Stop Loading work the same way as the Stop and Reload buttons on Navigator's main toolbar: When you're downloading a Web page, you can pause in the middle and change your mind (Stop Loading), or start over if something goes wrong (Reload). Show Images is something you don't have to think about if you're using Communicator, because it is a graphical program. Refresh empties your disk cache, or short-term memory, which some Web page authors recommend doing when visiting their sites.

5 Page Source shows you what the source code of a Web page looks like—all HTML and programming details you don't need to learn to use Composer. (When you discover a really stunning Web page and want to know just how they did it, checking the source code can help satisfy your curiosity.)

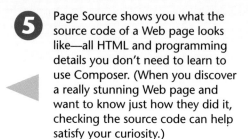

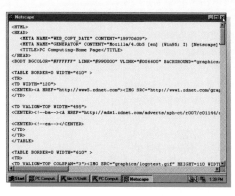

How to Use Composer's Insert Menu

When you're building your own Web pages from scratch, you use the Insert menu to introduce new elements into your Web page quickly and easily. First, position the cursor at the point on your page where you want to insert a background, image, link, line, table, or HTML tag, and then select the appropriate command from the Insert menu—it's a snap.

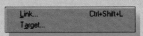

1 The Link option lets you choose between connecting to another page in your Web site or to another site altogether. Target is a navigation function that you'd use on a long Web page.

● Composer provides many tools to help you create professional-looking Web pages. For example, when you use the New Line Break and Break below Image(s) features to arrange elements on your page instead of pressing Enter to add space, you ensure that your page will appear as you intended in other browsers. (Some other browsers do not recognize more than one hard return; if you add three returns between two images, let's say, then someone else using a different browser may see much less space between those images.)

5 New Line Break and Break below Image(s) allow you to begin a new line of text and to add space after an inserted image, respectively. It's a good idea to use these features to add space around elements in your Web page rather than pressing Enter.

2 Image lets you insert a picture. Horizontal Line inserts a long line or bar; this element is commonly used between different sections of a page.

3 Table lets you insert a whole table or individual rows, columns, or cells. Think of a table as a spreadsheet, and you can envision what each of these individual features would look like.

4 HTML Tag is an advanced feature for Web page authors who know HTML, the programming language used to build Web pages. Authoring software, like Netscape Composer, handles most HTML coding automatically.

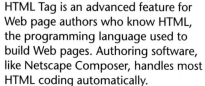

How to Use Composer's Format Menu

The Format menu is a lot like the Insert menu: Many of the capabilities and options listed here repeat options that are available through the main toolbar. However, the Format menu is also an easy way to establish your default text, page, link, and background colors; to assign various page properties, like custom color schemes; and to quickly clear your page of all applied styles if you change your mind in mid-design. Remember, you have to select part of your Web page for these tools and features to have the desired effect.

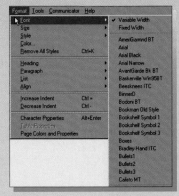

1 Font lets you establish a new main font for displaying text on your page, while Style lets you apply all kinds of effects, from bold and italic to strikethrough and blinking text.

6 Page Colors and Properties lets you customize Composer's default colors, background, and other built-in features.

2 Size lets you adjust the overall height and width of text by positive and negative increments, while Color lets you choose from a broad palette of basic and custom colors. Remove All Styles erases all styles you've applied, in case you change your mind and want to start from scratch.

3 Heading and Paragraph allow you to apply preset sizes and styles to specific areas or sections of your page text.

4 Align lets you change the alignment of page elements, while Increase Indent and Decrease Indent let you play with indenting by moving between two settings rather than four or five.

5 Character Properties and Table Properties open a Properties box where you can change many aspects of a page element in one convenient place.

How to Use Composer's Tools and Communicator Menus

You want to use Composer's spell checker to proof your Web page; you want to move among all five components of Communicator quickly; you want to look at your Address Book or bookmarks list: These are all examples of times you use the Tools and Communicator menus.

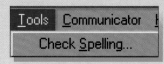

1 To access the spell checker, open the Tools menu. The spell checker is the only item on the list.

8 Last but not least, at the bottom of the Window menu is a numerical list of all open windows on your desktop. This is how you can quickly move among different windows and programs without opening and closing them to see what's underneath.

7 Java Console is an advanced Web page building feature you may use if you become an advanced Web page designer. Security Info will be discussed in Part 7.

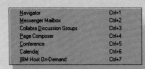

2 Moving on to the Communicator menu, Navigator opens a new Navigator window; Messenger Mailbox opens your e-mail; Collabra Discussion Groups opens your newsgroup postings; Page Composer opens a blank Web page; and Conference launches Communicator's long-distance calling program.

3 Show/Hide Component Bar determines the location of the button bar in the lower-right corner of Navigator's window.

4 Message Center opens your e-mail and newsgroups message center.

6 Bookmarks is a way to memorize and keep the URLs or addresses of Web pages you want to revisit.

5 Address Book is a list of e-mail addresses and newsgroups you write to frequently.

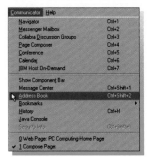

How to Use Composer's Help Menu

Composer's Help menu is a rich, detailed resource featuring all kinds of information and assistance. This is the place to learn more about Netscape and how they can provide you with assistance, consult technical information about Communicator, register Communicator, and more.

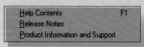

1 To read about Navigator's various features and capabilities, select Help Contents, Release Notes, and/or Product Information and Support. We will explore how to use Help Contents, or NetHelp, in one of the Projects at the end of the book.

7 About Communicator, the last item on the Help menu, is some legal jargon that you may or may not want to read.

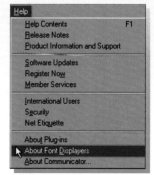

● Remember that you can use the help features listed on the Help menu for any of Communicator's components; this is the reason why all the Help menus in Navigator, Collabra, Messenger, and Composer look so similar.

6 About Font Displayers touches on questions concerning dynamic text and other, similar subjects.

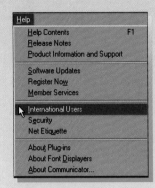

2 We already checked out Software Updates and Register Now in Part 1; Member Services contains the same type of information.

3 International Users contains specific information about using Communicator with languages other than English and in countries outside the United States.

4 Security is covered in Part 7, along with other issues. Net Etiquette provides newcomers to the Internet with an outline of basic online manners.

5 About Plug-ins is a list of audio, video, and other multimedia components already installed on your computer with Navigator.

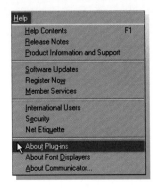

Building a Basic Web Page: Using the Page Wizard

Want to build a simple Web page quickly? Use the Page Wizard—it's simple and straightforward, like the setup Wizards you've encountered in previous parts. But when you're finished, you've created something new you can publish on the Internet as your own personal Web page.

1 Launch Communicator and log onto the Internet. Choose Composer from the Component bar, then click the New button on Composer's main toolbar.

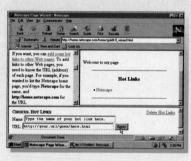

8 Scroll down to the next step and click the "add some hot links" link. Type **Netscape** in the Name text box and **http://home.netscape.com** in the URL text box. Click Apply to add these changes to the preview.

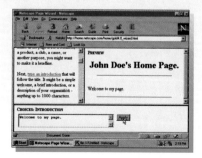

7 Use the scroll bar alongside the Instructions frame to proceed. Click the "type an introduction" link and, in the bottom frame, type **Welcome to my page** in the Introduction text box. Click Apply, and your introduction will be added to the preview.

● When you're using Composer's Page Wizard or any other kind of program that produces "ready-made" pages, be sure to check your spelling and other possible errors. If you make a mistake and don't catch it before you publish your page, you'll have to remake the entire page from scratch just to fix one thing.

2 The Create New Page dialog box appears. Choose From Page Wizard.

3 A new Navigator window will open. The Page Wizard is part of Netscape's home page divided into three frames. Scroll to the bottom of the upper-right frame and click Start.

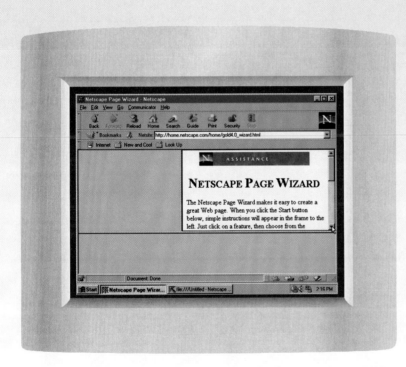

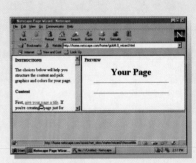

4 The Wizard's instructions appear in the upper-left frame, while a preview of your Web page appears in the upper-right frame. Click the "give your page a title" link in the upper-left frame.

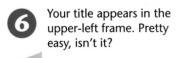

6 Your title appears in the upper-left frame. Pretty easy, isn't it?

5 Now the bottom frame comes into play: Click once in the title text box and type **John Doe's Home Page**. (Feel free to substitute your own name.) Click the Apply button when you're done.

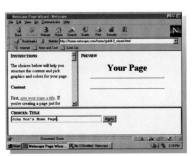

Building a Basic Web Page: Using the Page Wizard (Continued)

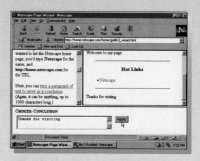

9 Scroll down to the next step and click the "conclusion" link. Type **Thanks for visiting** in the Conclusion text box and click Apply.

16 Your page will open in a new, lifesize Navigator window just as you created it. To save it, open Navigator's File menu and choose Save As. Windows will present you with the Save As dialog box, where you can name this page and save it to your hard drive.

15 You have just finished your page; look it over and make any changes, then click the Build button.

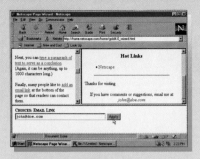

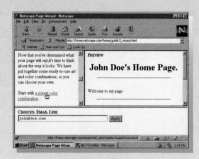

10 Last, click the "add an email link" link and type your e-mail address in the text box provided. Click Apply—now you've finished the text.

11 Now the Wizard lets you add some color. Because you're just practicing, click the "preset color combination" link to open an array of preestablished choices.

12 Each combination is made up of four colors: the background, text, and two links choices. Choose cadet blue in the middle of the color bar.

14 Now click the "choose a horizontal rule style" link and select a rule style. The second option also moves, so click that one.

13 Click the "choose a bullet style" link and select the bullet that moves.

Building a Basic Web Page: Using a Template

In this lesson, you learn how to create a basic page by using templates from Netscape's Web site. Rather than creating something from lists of preset choices, as with the Page Wizard, you can modify existing sample pages using Composer's tools. Later on in this section you'll learn how to make a page totally from scratch.

1 Launch Communicator and log onto the Internet. Choose Composer from the Component bar. Click the New button on Composer's main toolbar to open the Create New Page dialog box. Choose From Template.

8 ...and the text is gone.

FYI

● The Internet is a dynamic, ever-changing place. The template you use today may be gone tomorrow, but the way you use a template will not change.

7 ...click the Cut button on the main toolbar...

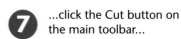

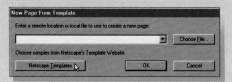

2 In the New Page From Template dialog box, click the Netscape Templates button. A new Navigator window will appear, displaying your choice of templates on Netscape's Web site.

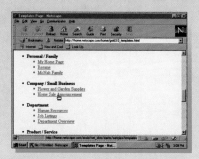

3 Scroll down and choose the template link Home Sale Announcement. You're going to create a simple business page.

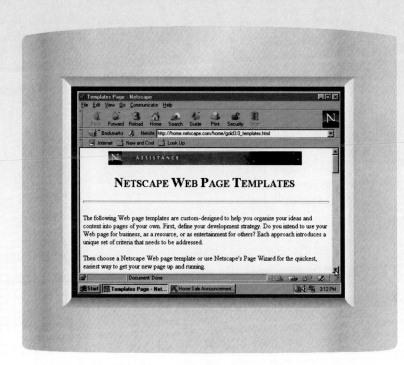

4 This is a mock-up of a Web page advertising a house for sale. Open the File menu and choose Edit Page. This will close Navigator and import this template into Composer.

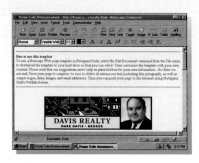

5 This template looks mostly the same, but there's a cursor blinking to the right of the broker's picture. You can place this cursor anywhere on the page just by pointing and clicking with the mouse.

6 Use the mouse to highlight all the instructions at the top of the page, then release the mouse key...

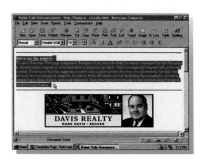

Building a Basic Web Page: Using a Template (Continued)

9 Now there are two horizontal bars at the top of your page. Click the top one once to select it, then press the Delete key. Looks better now, don't you think?

15 In the Windows Save As dialog box, name the template page **newpage.html** and click Save. You'll come back to it in a Project later on, so don't forget what it's called.

14 Press Ctrl+W to close the document, and click Yes when Composer asks if you want to save it.

10 Let's say this is the listing for your house. Highlight the words "Showcase Home of the Month," open the Font Color drop-down list, and select the navy blue square. Now roll the cursor away and click once—the text has changed color.

11 Now scroll down and highlight the words "Insert your address." Type in **123 Main Street**. Now highlight it again and open the Font Size drop-down list; select the 24 point setting.

Features at-a-glance

- *2500 square feet / 1.5 acre lot*
- *3 bedrooms, 2 full baths*
- *cedar-lined closet*
- *2 car detached garage*
- *security system*
- *priced to sell*

12 Scroll down to the list of the house's features at-a-glance; there's one missing. Position the cursor at the end of the second bullet, after the word "baths," and press Enter. A new bullet appears; type **cedar-lined closet**, and see that it's automatically italicized to match.

13 Finally, scroll down to the words "insert your company name" and highlight them with the mouse. Type in **ABC Realty, 555-1212**, and you're finished.

- *3 bedrooms, 2 full baths*
- *cedar-lined closet*
- *2 car detached garage*
- *security system*
- *priced to sell*

ABC Realty, 555-1212
For more information contact Davis Realty

Building a Basic Web Page: Using Composer's Tools and Menus

If you like to do things all by yourself, you can create a Web page entirely from scratch in Composer. In this exercise, you use only Composer's tools and menus and nothing else.

1 Launch Communicator and log onto the Internet. Choose Composer from the Component bar. Click the New button on Composer's main toolbar to open the Create New Page dialog box. Choose Blank Page.

8 Now let's insert an image. Press Enter a few times to make some room, then click the Image button on the main toolbar. Composer will prompt you to save your page, so name it **homepage** and click Save.

● Here's the most important tip you'll ever get regarding making your own Web pages: Save often. Save every five minutes; save every time you finish a paragraph or a feature. Otherwise you'll forget to save entirely, and if there's a power surge or your computer crashes, everything will be lost.

7 Now when you unhighlight the text, you'll see that it's green, italicized, and centered.

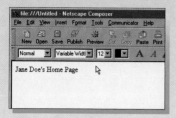

2 Type **Jane Doe's Home Page** right where the cursor appears. It will be small, black, and aligned to the left margin—in other words, boring.

3 Highlight what you just typed and open the Font Size menu. Select a point size of 18. Now your title is larger and easier to read.

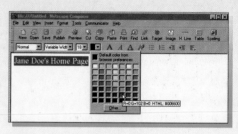

4 Next, leave the text highlighted and open the Font Color drop-down list. Select a dark green.

5 Move on to the Italic button on the same toolbar and click it.

6 And finally, click the Alignment button and select the second option, Center.

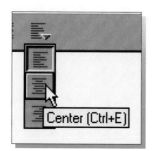

Building a Basic Web Page: Using Composer's Tools and Menus (Continued)

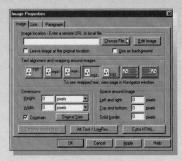

9 The Image Properties dialog box will appear to ask you for the image's file name. Click the Choose File button to browse your hard drive.

16 Now deselect the text. You've successfully completed the link and your Web page. Press Ctrl+S to save your work, and then pat yourself on the back.

15 The Character Properties dialog box appears; select the Link tab. Type **newpage.html** in the proper text box and click OK.

10 There's already a usable image on your desktop: the white house from the page you created with a template simply called "house." Double-click on it.

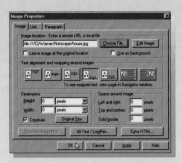

11 The pathway to the image will appear in the Image Properties dialog box. Click OK.

12 Now the house image (with the pretty green lawn that matches your page title) appears in the center of your Web page. Position the cursor between the title and the image.

14 The last thing to do is link the words "for sale" to the sale listing page you created in the previous exercise. Highlight the words "for sale" and click the Link button on the main toolbar.

13 Now press Enter a few more times to move the image a little further down the page, and type **This is my home and it's for sale.** Get it? Home page? Just a little Web humor.

How to Publish Your Web Pages on the Internet

You've spent a lot of time and effort creating your Web masterpieces, and you want to show them to the world. In this exercise, you'll learn how to upload your Web pages to your Internet service provider using Composer—no other software required.

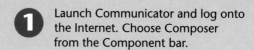 **1** Launch Communicator and log onto the Internet. Choose Composer from the Component bar.

5 Composer will contact your ISP and begin transmitting the files for you—not just the pages themselves, but any other files or images related to those pages as well—just by publishing your page once.

● Before you upload your Web pages, do one last thorough check for links that don't work and spelling errors. Also, take another look at the colors you chose. It's very disappointing to see your page online and not like it—or to have someone point out a mistake.

2 Click the Open button on the main toolbar to find your Web page on your hard drive (it's called **homepage** remember?). Double-click on it to select it in the Open dialog box.

3 Now you're ready to upload your Web page. Click the Publish button on the main toolbar to open the Publish dialog box.

4 The information about your Web page is already typed in where it should be, but you need to add the FTP address of your Internet service provider, your user name, and your password. If you don't have this information at hand, call your ISP. Otherwise, click OK when you're done.

PART 7

Building on the Basics: Multimedia, Security, and More

IN THIS SECTION YOU'LL LEARN

Using QuickTime: Movies

As the Internet becomes more popular, the average user's connection speed continues to increase. This means more and more Web sites are making use of video, because more and more people have the hardware and the capability to view movies. In this section, we'll surf to a handful of Web sites that use various types of movies to demonstrate how Navigator uses QuickTime.

Go to: http://www.mcp.com/people/mulder/emma

1 After you've launched Navigator and logged onto the Internet, click once in the Location box and type **http://www.mcp.com/people/mulder/emma**. Press Enter.

8 You can also use the Forward or Reverse buttons in the lower right corner of the player box to see the clip again, or click and drag the horizontal slider.

● Remember that having a fast connection solves only half the problem where speed and the Internet are concerned. As more people log on to the so-called information superhighway, overall speed has gotten slow, particularly during peak hours (for most areas, between 6:00 P.M. and 11:00 P.M.) This is why downloading the same movie can take three minutes or six minutes, and there's little you can do about it.

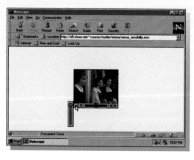

7 If you can't hear the soundtrack, click once and hold down the volume button. A vertical slider will appear that allows you to turn up the sound.

3 Sure enough, at the bottom there's a link to movie clips. Click once on "She Moves."

2 Welcome to a Web site devoted to Emma Thompson, the international movie star. Fan sites like these often feature lots of multimedia, so click once on "The Gallery."

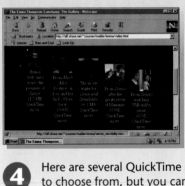

4 Here are several QuickTime movies to choose from, but you can immediately see why connection speed is so important: the smallest movie file, on the end at right, is 685K! Click it once to view it.

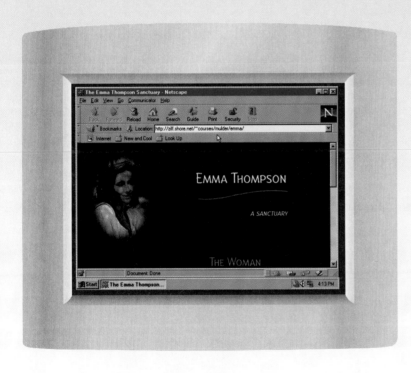

5 Navigator brings up the QuickTime symbol in the middle of a blank window while the movie downloads—you can watch the progress in the lower left corner. (Have patience.)

6 When the movie is completely downloaded, you'll see it appear in a player box—those buttons beneath the movie work just like those on a tape or CD player. Click the Play button once, and the movie will begin.

Using LiveVideo: The Return of Movies

Why does Navigator come with two movie plug-ins? Because not all movies are saved in the same format, and not every plug-in can play every movie. Fortunately both LiveVideo and QuickTime are already installed with Navigator, so you don't have to install anything or adjust your Preferences to make both work.

1 After you've launched Navigator and logged onto the Internet, click once in the Location box and type **www.evita-themovie.com**. Press Enter.

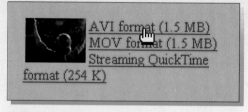

7 To replay, use the Back button on the main toolbar and click the AVI link again.

In the spirit of a free Internet environment, most (but not all) Web sites with original, copyright-protected content like movie clips and sound bites will allow you to download one copy of a file for your personal use. That is, you can put it on your personal Web site, period. This is very different from putting a movie or sound file on a commercial site or otherwise using it in a business, profit-earning situation. So if you're a Web site designer or you're involved with building your company's Web site, be aware of the copyright and other legal restrictions involved in using online material.

6 LiveVideo plays this movie in the upper left corner of the Navigator window—you can't click and drag it to the center, nor can you pause it or adjust the volume. In this example, the whole Navigator window is reduced to make viewing easier.

2 Welcome to the official Evita Web site. Click the oval picture in the center of the page, and you'll be taken to the main directory page.

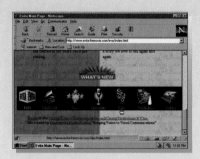

3 Use the slider bar (to the right of the screen) to scroll down to the main menu at the bottom of the page. Click Clips once.

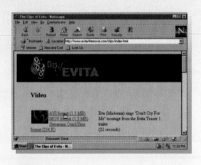

4 Take a close look at these two clips, and the need for more than one video plug-in becomes clear: each clip is saved in three different formats: AVI, MOV, and QuickTime (which we've already covered). AVI is a Windows-specific, non-QuickTime movie format, so click the AVI link to the top clip once.

5 LiveVideo will only start up when the clip is completely downloaded, so you'll look at a blank Navigator window till the movie is ready to play. (This clip is longer than the last one, so you'll still need patience.)

Using LiveAudio: Sounds and Music

Y ou'll find sound being used in many interesting ways on the Internet today. There are background music and sound effects, as well as the bits and pieces of music, concert recordings, movie dialog, and sound effects you can download. LiveAudio is the Navigator standard for playing downloadable sounds, and you'll see how it works in this section.

1 After you've launched Navigator and logged onto the Internet, click once in the Location box and type **www.atlanticrecords.com**. Press Enter.

7 When the Stop button shines green, the song is over. Click Play to hear the song again.

● Not all sounds, songs, and video clips that are downloadable from the Web are actual files you get to keep. The song you listened to in this exercise, for example, is a one-time-only file—you can listen to it during your current surfing session, but after you quit Navigator you'll have to download it all over again.

6 A tiny player box appears in the gray window, with Stop, Play, and Pause buttons. The horizontal slider controls the volume, indicated by the graduated green scale just beneath it. Click the middle Play button once, and listen to the music.

2 This is the official Atlantic Records home page, featuring sound files from just about every Atlantic artist. Click Artists & Music once to get to the alphabetical index.

3 Jewel is a personal favorite, so click the Jewel link once. There's a "music" link in the middle of the page—click it once.

4 Just as with the video clips you've viewed, you have a choice among three file formats. Choose the AIFF of "You Were Meant For Me" by clicking it once.

5 A small Navigator window appears with a shaded gray Netscape logo inside—this is where the sound file will appear once it's completely downloaded.

Using Virtual Reality: Live3D

Virtual reality is one of the newest and most fascinating aspects of the online community, and some of the most interesting, cutting-edge Web sites are including it. In this section, you'll visit Cybertown, USA—a futuristic community that's being expanded every day as more and more designers add their own virtual "neighborhoods" to adjoin Colony City. So grab your mouse—the only thing you'll need to navigate in 3D—and let's get started.

1 After you've launched Navigator and logged onto the Internet, click once in the Location box and type **www.cybertown.com**. Press Enter.

8 To visit other areas of Cybertown, use the Back button on the main toolbar to return to the map. But most important, have fun!

7 The only real control you need is your mouse, and it may take a little getting used to. You can go in any direction and you may find yourself flying without realizing how you left the ground.

● It is very easy to become disconcerted in a virtual reality world, even if you're just looking at a computer screen—even the cursor disappears as you're floating around, so there's little to anchor you to the real world. If you get dizzy or overwhelmed, look away from the computer until you get your bearings again. Once you get accustomed to the controls, you'll find yourself less and less affected.

2 Ready to become a virtual tourist? Scroll down the main page to the distinctive 3DVR item on the bulleted list of options—click once on the purple button.

3 Scroll down the 3D Virtual Reality page to the Cybertown Main Town area of the page and click the "here" link once. (There's a lot to do here so there's a lot to get through.)

4 Click once on the Map icon. We're getting there.

5 Here's the main map of Cybertown, with nine different areas to choose from. They all look interesting, but click once on Main Town.

6 Don't touch the mouse until the whole view has loaded up—you'll be tempted to jump in, but you need to see everything (including the toolbar along the bottom) before you decide where you want to go.

Using Animation and Other Effects: Shockwave

Shockwave is a cool little plug-in that greatly increases Navigator's basic multimedia capabilities. Web designers use Shockwave to create all kinds of effects, from the simple glows and shadowing (PC Computing uses Shockwave on your default home page) to all kinds of sophisticated video and animation techniques. To show you all the things Shockwave can do, we're going to visit Macromedia's Web site (the people who created Shockwave) and have a look at their Gallery.

Go to: www.macromedia.com/shockwave

1 After you've launched Navigator and logged onto the Internet, click once in the Location box and type **www.macromedia.com/shockwave**. Press Enter.

6 Studio Archetype, otherwise known as Clement Mok Designs, uses Shockwave on their Web site to create a streamlined multimedia interface. Check it out at **www.studioarchetype.com**.

● It may take a moment for a Shockwave file to load up completely, just like it takes time for a movie or sound file to download.

2 We're headed for the Shockwave Gallery to look at all the things Shockwave can do, so click the "See the Gallery" link once. This brings up the main Gallery page.

3 Here are some great examples of what Shockwave can do as listed on the Staff Picks page, plus the URLS where you can find them. At **www.mainquad.com/flash-cards**, you can assemble your own online cards with covers, music, and inside messages you customize.

4 Choose the Shockwave version of **www.id4movie.com/gateway** and view a promotional site for the movie Independence Day that's overrun with Shockwave features: animation, blinking buttons and bars, and the personalized comic book adventure for users who register (a page of it is shown here).

5 Having a bad day? Take it out on your "favorite" celebrity at **slugfest.kaizen.net**. Choose from Bullies, Meanies, and Wussies. Virtual satisfaction only, of course.

How to Install a Plug-In: RealAudio

Sometimes you'll download a file or try something on a Web site, and a dialog box will pop up saying "Sorry." It will effectively say, "You don't have the right plug-in to do what you want to do." What do you do in this situation? Go find the plug-in you need, download it, and install it. That's what you'll learn to do in this section with a popular audio plug-in called RealAudio.

1 Launch Navigator and log onto the Internet. Let's assume you want to listen to music on TheDJ, one of the sites you can visit in the first Project, but you don't have RealAudio installed. Click once in the Location bar and type **realaudio**. This takes you to Progressive Networks' site where you can download RealAudio for free.

8 You'll have to exit Navigator to install RealAudio, so open the File pull-down menu and choose Exit. The RealAudio installation file you saved to your desktop is called **ra32_30**. Double-click it to kick off the installation process.

7 The Saving Location dialog box appears, and you can watch the file download till it's done.

● You should be just as careful with the volume level when playing music as when using Conference: Your computer is not an expensive stereo system, and you can damage your speakers by jacking up the volume.

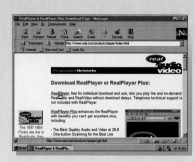

2 Click once on the link that reads "RealPlayer," the no-frills plug-in you want to add to Navigator.

3 Click the "download now" link under RealAudio Player. It's free for individual use.

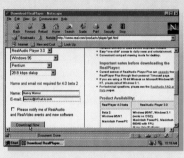

4 Scroll down to the form and fill it out according to your computer platform, operating systems (or OS) and your connection speed. Click once on the "Download Now" button when you're done.

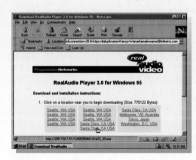

5 Choose a download site location that's appropriate (close to where you are geographically) and click its link.

6 A Save As dialog box will appear, asking you where you want to save the RealAudio installation file. The desktop is always a good choice. Click Save when you're finished, and the download will begin.

How to Install a Plug-In: RealAudio (Continued)

9 Here's what the first screen of the RealAudio setup program looks like. You're going to perform a standard installation, so click Next.

16 Now click the logo in the middle of the screen, and a new separate player window will appear. Choose a station/music type (everything from country to swing to reggae) and the music will automatically begin to play.

15 Click once in the Location box and type **thedj**. You're back at TheDJ.com, a programmable online music source. Click once on the big key in the middle of the screen.

10 Agree to the Licensing Agreement and click Next. Now enter your name, organization (if needed) and a valid e-mail address. Click Next when you're finished.

11 RealAudio works best on 28.8Kbps connections or better, but if you're using a slower modem choose the correct option from the pull-down menu here. Click Next when you're finished.

12 The setup program will choose a Destination; click Next to accept it. Then it will ask you to choose which browser(s) on your computer should be set up to run RealAudio. Check or uncheck the appropriate box and click Next.

13 Finally, the setup program will indicate your default browser (Navigator, of course) and you can click Finish.

14 Installation was successful! After the "thank you" test finishes (you'll hear and see a recorded, "Thanks") let's relaunch Navigator and try it out.

How to Tell if a Site is Secure: The Security Button

In this section, you'll become familiar with the ways Navigator lets you know you're looking at a secure Web site. This also serves as a reintroduction to some of the security features you've passed along the way as you've gone through this book.

1 First, launch Communicator and log onto the Internet. Wait for Navigator to open your default home page (PC Computing's home page, unless you've recustomized this setting) and then click the Security button on the main toolbar.

8 The last Security menu category is Cryptographic Modules, a mouthful of a phrase that just means "Here's a list of what Netscape uses to encrypt your e-mail and newsgroup postings if that's what you want."

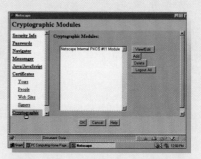

FYI

● The certificate information you read on the Document Info page relates to a site certificate, a security verification that works like your driver's license when you write a check. It is a unique ID that lets you know you're dealing with a reputable, genuine company and not someone who wants to steal your information.

● In the final version of Communicator, Netscape also says that the bar along the top edge of Navigator's window will change color if you're viewing a secure site. Right now (during beta release) this edge is always dark blue, but watch for this feature to change.

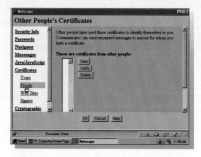

7 In a nutshell, certificates let you send and receive encrypted messages, but you have to have one yourself and Navigator has to keep a record of other people's certificates, too. Click the People sublist link to see an example. This is where Navigator would be keeping track of others' certificates if you'd been exchanging encrypted messages with them.

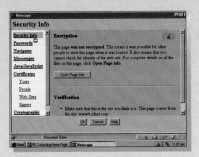

2 A new Netscape window will appear—this is the Security Info center where you can learn all you ever want to know about the security of a site you're visiting. Security Info, the first category listing on the menu at the left side, deals with Encryption (whether or not a Web site needs to be decoded before it can be read) and Verfication (the URL listed here is www4.zdnet.com, so yes, you're in the right place).

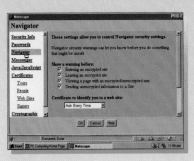

3 Click Navigator on the left side and your Navigator Security information will appear: when you want Navigator to warn you, when you'll want your personal certificate to identify you (you'll register for one in the next exercise), and some advanced security or SSL configuration information.

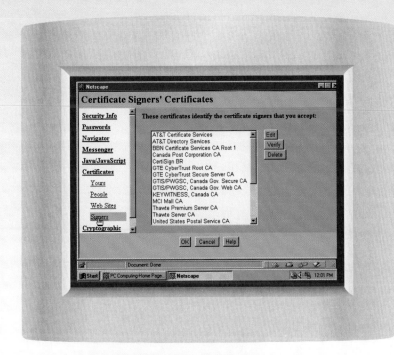

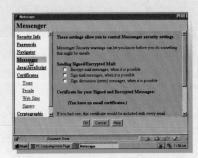

4 Click Messenger on the left side and your Messenger Security information will appear: when/if you want Messenger to encrypt or sign your outgoing e-mail and newsgroup postings; more tantalizing information about that personal certificate; and S/MIME configuration choices.

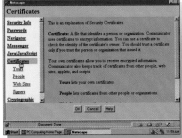

6 Click Certificates for an explanation of what certificates are.

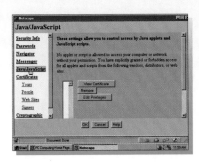

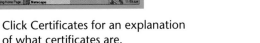

5 Click Java/JavaScript on the left side and more Web page Security information will appear. If you want to deny certain people permission to access your information using a script or applet, this is the place to do so.

PROJECT 1
The Surfing Safari: More with Navigator

Here's the chance to practice the basic Navigator and Web surfing techniques you learned throughout this book. In this exercise you'll surf to many exotic locales and practice with the toolbar and the pull-down menus. You'll start with the PC/Computing home page; venture to sites about sports, music, food, travel, movies, and art; and finally wind up back at the PC/Computing site where you started. It's a sort of scavenger hunt via Navigator. To begin, launch Navigator and proceed to the first step. Happy surfing!

Since you reset your default home page to PC/Computing in an earlier chapter, you should be looking at the PC/C home page. Roll the cursor to the What's Hot icon and double-click it.

Scroll down the What's Hot! page and double-click on **1,001 Best Web Sites** under Cool Stuff.

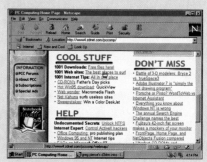

Scroll down the menu frame on the left side till you find the **Sports** button. Double-click it.

A Sports menu page will load in the center frame. Double-click **Extreme Sports**.

5

Again, the center frame menu will change. Double-click **Get Lost Adventure Magazine.** Rock climbing, anyone?

6

Now use the Back button to return to the 1,001 Best Web Sites page and click the **Fun and Weird** button. Choose the **Charlie's Angels home page** for a little retro.

7

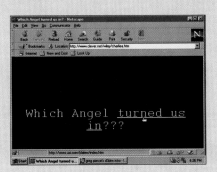

Now that we've revisited the seventies, use the Back button again to return to the Fun and Weird. Click **Electro Magnetic Poetry** to get creative.

8

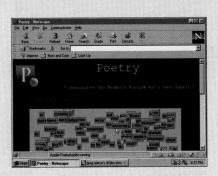

Had enough weird for now? Then let's do a little foreign travel.

9

Click in the Location box, type **www.indonesia today.com/home.html** and press Return. The tropical rainforests are supposed to be very lovely, so let's check them out: click **Tropical Forests** once.

10

Now you're curious about ecotourism, aren't you? Click in the Location box, type **www.divetravel.com/Ecotrav.html** and press Return.

11

Maybe you want to travel closer to home, though: Click the Location box, type **cityview.com/sanfrancisco**, and press Return.

Continue to next page ☞

PROJECT 1

Continued from previous page

12

Here's everything you need to know about traveling in the Bay Area. Now that we're back in North America, let's check in on current events.

13

Click in the Location box, type **www. pathfinder. com** and press Return. Pathfinder has dozens of magazines and other publications to choose from.

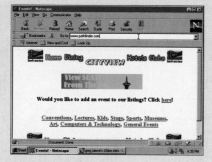

14

Find the **Entertainment Weekly** link (just about the middle of the page) and click it once. You'll go to the Entertainment Online site. Click the **Movie Central** link for movie reviews.

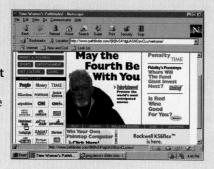

15

Maybe new music is more interesting. Click in the Location box, type **www. thedj.com** and press Return to listen to more than 48 channels of commercial-free music in your category of choice.

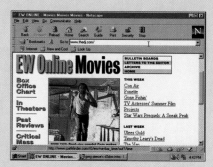

16

Use the Back button to return to Pathfinder and click the **Net Culture** link. Read about the latest news, the hottest sites, and technical stuff in cyberspace.

17

Hungry? Click in the Location box, type **www. dorothylane. com** and press Return to order in from the Dorothy Lane Market—grocers to the world on the World Wide Web.

18

If your need to feed is more immediate, Click in the Location box, type **www.txicp. com/rdn** and

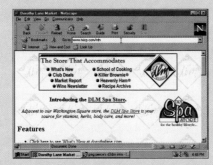

press Return for pizza, Mexican, American, whatever, delivered to your door. (Only if you live in southeast Texas, though.)

19

Now you're probably thirsty. Click in the Location box, type **www. snapple.com**,

and press Return. Now that you've refueled, let's keep surfing.

20

Click the Location box, type **www. sptimes.com/ Treasures**, and press Return. This is

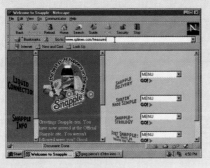

the lobby of a permanent museum exhibit of artifacts from the Russian czars. (Didn't you have a suit of armor when you were a child, too?)

21

The last stop on our virtual tour is Women's Wire. Click in the Location box, type **www. women.com**, and press Return for a

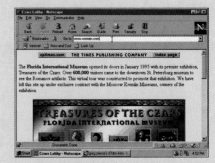

brief look at the world of modern women.

22

Finally, use the Home button on the main toolbar to return to where you started: the

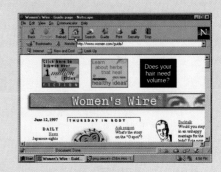

PC/Computing home page. You've just successfully completed your first long-distance journey into cyberspace, so it's time to explore more of Navigator.

Advanced E-mail Features: More with Messenger

R eady to explore Netscape Messenger a little further? In this Project you'll practice what you learned about Messenger, and use some new, advanced features, namely folders, threads, filters, and how to send URLs in e-mail messages. So if you're ready, let's get started by launching Navigator and logging on to the Internet.

1 First, click the Open/Close tab on the left of the taskbar so the taskbar will float independently on your desktop. Then click Mailbox to launch Messenger.

2 Open the Drafts folder on the Inbox menu by rolling the cursor down to Drafts and clicking once.

3 We're going to use the e-mail message you saved here in Part 3, so double-click "re: test message" to open it.

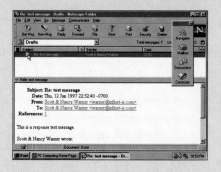

4 Now open the Message pull-down menu and choose Attach Web Page. A dialog box will appear, showing all the documents saved on your computer desktop; double-click **newpage** to attach it.

5 Next, open the Insert pull-down menu and choose Link. A Properties dialog box will appear; in the Link Source field, type **Here's a link to Netscape's home page**. Also, in the second Link To field, type **http://home.netscape.com**. Click OK.

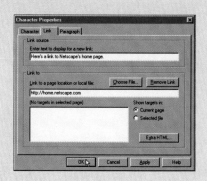

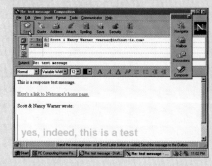

6 Now your e-mail message contains a link to Netscape's home page. Click the Send button on the main toolbar to send it immediately, then use the Folders pull-down menu to return to your Inbox.

7

Let's use some of Messenger's Folder management features. Click the Message Center button on the right side of the Inbox window, and the Message Center will appear. Open the File pull-down menu and choose New Folder. We're going to create a new, customized e-mail folder to practice with.

8

A User Prompt dialog box will appear; type **Test** in the field as shown here and click the OK button once.

9

Your new folder appears in your Message Center window, as a subfolder in your Outbox.

10

Now click the Get Msg button on the main toolbar to retrieve the test message you just sent. Messenger will ask you for your password, so type it in and your new mail will be downloaded.

11

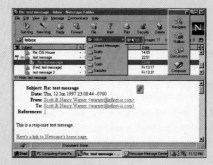

Click the test message once to highlight it, then click the File button on the main toolbar. Roll the cursor down the choices until you find the Test folder and click once. You've just learned how to sort and save your e-mail messages to different folders.

12

Next, let's explore some ways you can automatically arrange incoming e-mail for easier reading. You're still in your Inbox, so open the View pull-down menu and choose Sort. A submenu will automatically pop up; choose By Subject.

13

The e-mail in your Inbox is now arranged alphabetically by subject, and it will automatically be sorted this way every time you check it. (Go back to the View pull-down menu and resort by Date if you prefer your e-mail to be sorted chronologically.)

Continue to next page ☞

P R O J E C T   2

Continued from previous page

14

It can also be useful to sort and manage e-mail by thread or subject. First, click once on a message in your Inbox with the subject "test message." Now open the Edit pull-down menu and choose Select Thread.

15

As you can see, Messenger has not only selected the original message but also all other messages in the Inbox with the same subject heading. For the sake of this exercise, let's say you're not interested in reading test messages—open the Message pull-down menu and select Ignore Thread. Now if you use the Next and Backtrack buttons on the main toolbar to read through all your messages, starting at the top, Messenger will skip over e-mail with "test message" in the subject line.

16

You can also designate as first priority any messages concerning a specific subject. To do this, click once on a message in your Inbox with the subject you're most interested in—use "test message" again for purposes of this exercise. Open the Message pull-down menu and choose Watch Thread.

17

Now open the View menu, choose Sort, and resort your Inbox contents by Priority.

18

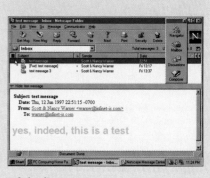

Messenger reshuffles the contents of your Inbox and places all e-mail with a subject of "test message" at the top of the list.

19

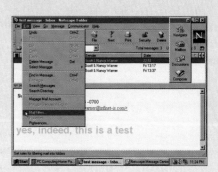

If you want to establish a priority list for all incoming e-mail of all different subjects, you can use mail filters. Open the Edit pull-down menu and choose Mail Filters.

20

The Mail Filters dialog box will appear; click the New button once to get started, and a Filter Rules dialog box will open.

21

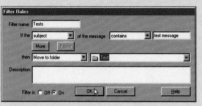

The Filter Rules dialog box gives you many ways to sort and prioritize your incoming e-mail—in this example, a filter named Tests will automatically move any new e-mail with "test message" contained in the subject to the Test folder. (Have a look at the other available options by opening the different pull-down menus.) Finally, turn the Filter on using the "switch" at the bottom (marked Off and On), and click OK once.

22

The filter called Tests that you just created now appears in the Mail Filters dialog box at the top of the list. Later on, if you want to edit or change some of this filter's features, you can use the Edit Filter button, or use the Delete Filter button to get rid of it altogether. For now, click OK.

23

Now test your new filter by clicking the Compose button on the main toolbar and sending yourself a test message with **test message** typed in the Subject line. Click the Send button when you're finished.

24

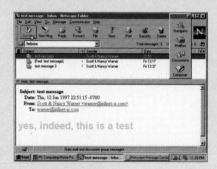

Click the Get Msg button on the main toolbar to download your new test message. You might want to wait a moment or so to make sure your Internet service provider receives and delivers it.

25

Now when you open your Test folder, you'll find that Messenger has automatically routed your new message there, which proves that your Mail Filter is working properly.

PROJECT 3

Advanced Inbox Features: More with Collabra

In this section, you'll explore Netscape Conference and Netscape Collabra a little more thoroughly by learning how to build up the Address Book. First, as always, launch Communicator and log onto the Internet so we can get started.

1

From the Navigator window, access your Address Book by opening the Communicator pull-down menu and choosing Address Book.

2

You're going to add some names and other information to your Address Book to make it multifunctional. Click once on the New Card button.

3

The New Card dialog box appears. On the Name page, type in the person's first name, last name, and e-mail address.

4

Now click the Netscape Conference page tab. You can establish either an e-mail address or a Netscape Conference DLS (directory listing or netphone number) in the Conference Address Location box. For this person, type in their e-mail address and check the Address choice. Click OK.

5

Now you've added someone to your Address Book with an e-mail address for a Conference number. Next, let's add someone with a DLS or netphone number.

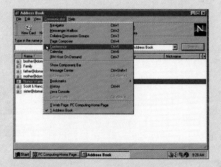

6

You should be in the Address Book window. Open the Communicator pull-down menu and choose Conference.

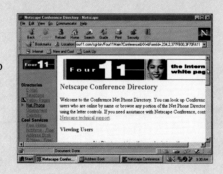

7

Click the Web Phonebook button to search Netscape's online Directory of Conference users. For the purposes of this exercise, search for your own DNS entry.

8

Remember that a person will only be listed on Netscape's Conference Phonebook if they choose to be during Conference's setup session, and only if they're online using Conference. Click the first letter of your last name once.

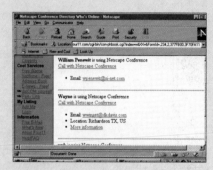

9

No such luck—if you followed the Setup Wizard instructions given earlier, you won't find yourself listed here because you didn't type in your last name first. Try searching under the first letter of your first name instead.

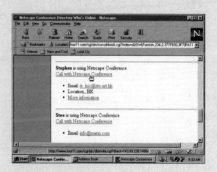

10

Success—click your own name once.

Continue to next page ☞

PROJECT 3

Continued from previous page

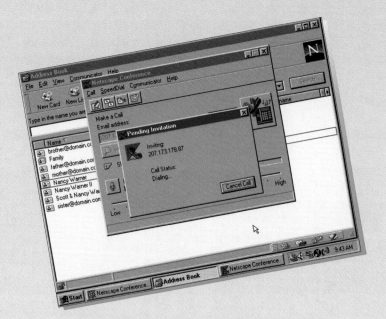

13

Click and drag the mouse across the DLS number in Conference's Location box and press Ctrl+C. This copies the number and saves it in Communicator's memory.

14

Now return to the Address Book, and click the New Card button again.

15

Click once on the Netscape Conference page tab, then click once in the Conference Address Location box. Press Ctrl+V to paste the DLS number into the window, and specify that it's a Netscape Conference DLS.

11

Conference will launch a call, but naturally the line will be busy. Click OK—you've actually accomplished your goal.

12

Despite the fact that your call did not go through, the DLS number remains in the Location box. This is the number you'll put in your Address Book instead of an e-mail address.

16

Don't forget to click once on the Name page tab and type in your first name, last name, and e-mail address. Click OK when you're finished to save the entry.

20

There will also be a way for you to add newsgroup list names to your Address Book for easily addressing posts, so the real lesson here is: it pays to spend some time building up your Address Book. It is a versatile feature you can use to make Collabra, Messenger, and Conference work more efficiently.

17

Now you have two entries in your Address Book, complete with e-mail addresses and Conference phone numbers.

18

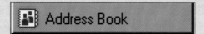

Making such Address Book entries enables you to call using either the Address Book button on Conference's main window...

19

... or the Call button on the Address Book main toolbar (in this picture, Conference is not launched so the Call button is shaded, or inactive.)

CREDITS

The World Wide Web would be nothing without content, which is why we offer special thanks to the following companies, individuals, universities, organizations, and other invaluable content providers whose Web sites are shown in *How to Use Netscape Communicator 4.0*:

Atlantic Records (Atlantic Records web site)

Russell K. Banz (Get Lost Adventure magazine)

BigBook, Inc. (BigBook is the nation's leading on-line yellow pages with listings for more than 16 million businesses and more than one million users per month)

clnet Inc. (Shareware.com)

Charlie's Angels home page

Cinergi (Evita, The Movie Official Web Site)

CityView

Cybertown Web Design (Courtesy of Cybertown, Inc.)

Dive Travel Magazine (DiveTravel)

Dorothy Lane Markets Inc. (Dorothy Lane Market Inc., Dayton, OH)

Four11 Corp. (Four11)

Guinness Brewing Co. (Guinness)

IndonesiaToday.com

Kaizen Works, Inc. (Celebrity Slugfest)

Lycos, Inc. (Lycos)

Macromedia, Inc. (The Shockwave Gallery)

The Main Quad (Flashcards)

Steve Mulder (The Emma Thompson Sanctuary)

Netscape Communications Corporation (Netscape Communications Corp.)

Progressive Networks (RealAudio)

Restaurant Delivery Network

Studio Archetype (StudioArchetype)

Used with permission by TheDJ Network (TheDJ is a registered trademark of Terraflex Data Systems, Inc.)

Time Warner Inc. (Pathfinder, Entertainment Weekly)

Electromagnetic Poetry by Prominence Dot Com, http://prominence.com/

Snapple

Rebecca Tapley (The Pyramid)

The Times Publishing Company (Treasures of the Czars)

VeriSign Corp. (VeriSign Digital ID page)

Wire Networks (Reprinted with permission from Women's Wire™ ©1997 http://www.women.com)

WSI Corporation (Intellicast)

Yahoo, Inc. (Yahoo!)

Ziff-Davis, Inc./ZD Net (PC/Computing magazine)

INDEX

BRIARCLIFF BRANCH 1/98/98